One Zero Eight

One Zero Eight

PARVIN D. SYAL

OTHER BOOKS

BY PARVIN D. SYAL

Poems from East Africa
Contributing Poet

Thus Says Kabir - "Listen O' Brethren Sadho!"
Chapter Contribution

Streams of Consciousness

African Quilt (with Harshi Syal Gill)

God Minus (with Harshi Syal Gill)

Dedicated to the memory of
DEV ANAND
(September 26, 1923-December 3, 2011)

FOREWORD

Parvin Syal is an extraordinary man and one of my oldest friends. Our friendship has stood the test of time. It is almost half a century since I set eyes on him while shooting for a film on a hill in San Fernando Valley in Los Angeles.

I was new to the US then and, after having spent six years behind the iron curtain (the USSR) in Moscow and having been brainwashed since early childhood by my father (a staunch Marxist) that there was no bigger villain in the world than the US of A, everything looked strange and frightening when I arrived there for the first time. I was nervous and like a fish out of water.

It was because of Parvin and his sister Harshi that my fear and nervousness gradually faded away as they took me home, to restaurants, for shopping and introduced me to the soul and spirit of America. As things turned out, by the end of my stay I was convinced that America was not the villain that had been painted for me but indeed a great country with a great people.

Over the years my friendship with Parvin deepened and I got to know him better. The man was full of surprises. Although of Kenyan origin (born and brought up in Kenya) and having lived most of his life in the US and away from India, he is more Indian than most Indians that I have known. While he was in Mumbai recently Parvin was busy with his sister Harshi visiting as many temples in the city as possible and imbibing the local culture. A lifetime lived in the US and earlier with his parents in Kenya had not made a dent on his 'Indian-ness'. In one of his poems called *Shani Shingnapur* we come across these lines:

> freshly bathed
> having cleansed myself
> adorned in a *dhoti*
> white
> prayer platter in hand
> marigolds to offer
> and oil to daub
> I await my turn
> in a line
> of devotees.

This is something few (and almost none of our generation) do nowadays. Albeit thousands of miles away from India, his roots are securely imbedded in Hindu culture and philosophy. He is truly a proud Indian. And, as Idowu Koyenikan has said: "Your pride for your country should not come after your country becomes great; your country becomes great because of your pride in it." Verily, India is great because of people like Parvin.

It was Parvin who brought about a renaissance in my life. I was aware of his expertise as a physician; that he is a superlative poet has come as a great surprise to me. I have read his poems avidly. His knowledge of Vedic philosophy is astonishing. I have read the Vedas sporadically but didn't understand the full meaning of the concept of God in them till I read these lines in his poem about Brahma:

        Brahma, the 1
        only 1 capable
        of internal combustion
        an engine
        self-fueled.
        hurtling towards
        future millennia
        creating at the will
        of a thought
        vibration,
        of a thought
        vocalized
        a cosmic ripple
        the static sheet
        of tranquility, tweaked
        shedding forth atoms
        elements elementary
        for creation, complex.

The first question I asked him when he told me about his collection
of poems was why it was called *One Zero Eight*. It was the exhibition
of my own ignorance. As he explains in one of his poems:

        In Vishnu envisages Brahma
        the Being Cosmic - *Vishwarupa*
        encompassing the universe whole.
        Vishnu with the one cosmic soul . . .
        Vishnu, master of vitality,
        of emotions and directions,
        vocations and planes of existence.
        Vishnu, Lord of the zodiac and
        the lunar asterisms - *nakshatras*,
        Vishnu, the master of 108 spirits.

All art, in the final analysis, is autobiographical, and this collection of poems is no exception. It is a spiritual journey of sorts and, to use a musical phrase, the diapason of his emotional range is astounding. Albeit a silent man not given to meaningless chatter, he is a living example of the saying "silent waters run deep", for in his poetry he shows as much interest in politics (*The Seat of Power*) as in travel; his poems are strewn with his observations about the many places in East Africa, India, the United States and across Europe that he has lived in and visited. One is struck by his powers of observation. In his poem about *Ajaccio Corsica* he speaks about:

> Vegetation diverse
> nurturing the bees
> producing honey
> distinct
> sweet, light amber -
> elixir of the hills
> dark, tinged with bitterness
> product of the foot-hills
> an accompaniment to liquor -
> medicinal gift from the gods.

Parvin has the eye of a painter. Often his descriptions have a pictorial quality that is fascinating and make one not just imagine the picture he is painting but also see it in technicolor, as this excerpt from one of his poems, *Shani Shingnapur,* illustrates:

> I used to dream
> of colors
> that would coat
> my imagination

an amalgam of
running rivulets
coalescing to form
a mellow mauve
a lilting lilac
a propitious purple
luminescence akin
a peacock's pride,
a violet plumage
of shades
unfamiliar to me.

I have always thought of doctors as pragmatic, down-to-earth people with hard boiled interiors. But I was mistaken. Although they are good at hiding their emotions physicians are, more often than not, more sensitive and emotional than us ordinary people. Parvin, for all his practical and quiet demeanor, is a very emotional man and of a romantic bent of mind, as one of his *Muse* poems illustrates:

When and why
did you become
prominent for me?
I know not the answer.
My eyes search for you.
My heart beats for you.
But the chasm
of silence between us
immense.

As I have said, Parvin is an extraordinary man. Also, he is a very endearing person. Behind the façade of cheerfulness and the ever-present smile lies a man of immense wisdom who has been through the grind and seen very hard times. To be born in a foreign clime (Kenya), as a migrant child, far away from the land of one's forefathers and yet to preserve its soul and spirit (thanks to his parents about whom he has written some very moving poems) and then to be uprooted and find himself in an entirely new world, suffer privation and hardship and build a new life for himself and the family is no mean accomplishment.

His has been a long journey. These poems are the essence of his varied experiences, his inner thoughts, the people he has met, his reactions to the events of his multi-faceted life and in them one can glean the soul and spirit of India.

To a man his native land
Is as unto the tree the root!
If there is labor fills no want
His deeds are doomed
His music mute.
(Henrik Ibsen)

All through these poems the music of Parvin's soul rings loud and clear! It is a music that both elevates and edifies, intrigues and moves, informs and entertains. Indeed, it rivets one with its inimitable beauty.

Parikshat Sahni
Mumbai, India

(Parikshat Sahni is a renowned Indian film and TV actor, with scores of movies and TV serials to his credit. In addition to writing the scripts for several TV serials, he recently published a book about his father, the iconic Balraj Sahni, titled *The Non-Conformist*.)

CONTENTS

CHAPTER A - BRAHMA

CHAPTER B - SHIVA

CHAPTER C - VISHNU

INTRODUCTION

The seven decades of my life have exposed me to experiences in various countries; they have exposed me to geographic and cultural aspects of different regions. They have exposed me to influences which, like the binary system of ones and zeros, gave rise to infinite permutations. Life, as a continuum, is a series of episodes and incidents - acts in which the dramatis personae appear as per pre-written lines. Recording life, however, is like writing a travelogue; many lanes and roads and tracks are traversed, but only a select few are mentioned.

The poems in this volume are a tribute to the 'what and the who and the where,' that inspired me through my journey - both public and personal. The latter included many muses to whom I offered my Ego in exchange for inspiration. Public influences were of the global kind, where I retained my Ego as a reference point for my gaze at the universe.

Are these poems auto-biographical? Most probably they are, but I have taken poetic license. Imagination over reality. Wishful thinking sometimes. There is a liberal usage of song titles and book titles and literary names, and other quotes which have become an integral part of the poems, and in the interest of retaining the flow of the words, I have not attributed them individually nor weighted them down with onerous quotation marks. Similarly names of historic persons are mentioned frequently.

There are, too, allusions to many Sanatana Dharmic concepts, on the foundation of which rest the amalgam of views of creation, preservation and destruction, represented theologically by Brahma, Vishnu and Shiva. I have relied on a vast array of texts on Indian religious and philosophic thought, but books by Indian mythologist, Dr. Devdutt Pattanaik have been a fount of knowledge for several years. I have relied on his perspicacity for some poems. Lin Yutang's *The Wisdom of India* has served as a sourcebook since my school-days.

I have also been touched by the Catholic faith; the Liverpool Metropolitan Cathedral has a unique place in my heart. The ancient druid method and covens worshipping at numerous places dotting the British Isles may seem antediluvian but the system still abides and I have borne witness to this practice.

In the African context the missionaries changed the religious and political topography of the land. Consequently, the Kenyans, particularly the Gikuyu, were victims of colonial brutality of a most unchristian kind.

Using all these as my springboard, I have incorporated in my poems wide-ranging citations of names, places, ideologies, etc. which can be easily researched by interested readers.

The 108 individual poems are offered at the altar of our collective human faith in one Supreme Being or Supreme force governing life.

How did I come up with the title? Was it an epiphany or realization; enlightenment or revelation? None! Just a thought that came to me in a dream, and on this occasion, I remembered it when I woke up.

In Hinduism - Sanatana Dharma as the ancients would call it - the significance of 108 is immense. The Upanishads, which expound the four Vedas, are 108 in number; there are 108 major pilgrimage sites in India.

The body has 108 subtle pressure points along the meridians where the conscious and material points meet, and at 108 degrees Fahrenheit, the body's organs start decomposing.

Vedic astrology has 27 *Nakshatras* - lunar asterisms - with each one having four parts, or *Padams*, totaling 108 segments, which minutely ascribe the planetary positions. Furthermore, the distance from the earth to the moon is 108 times the moon's diameter and to the sun it is 108 times the sun's diameter.

My interpretation of ONE ZERO EIGHT centers around the Trinity of the Hindu Godhead.

The number ONE signifies the Individual - *Ahamkara* or Ego. It also signifies Brahma - the Creator.

ZERO signifies *Shunya,* or nothingness - a "no end and no beginning." It signifies Shiva the destroyer, who has no origin nor end; just like the cycle of birth and death, which has no end nor beginning.

EIGHT is vast. It is infinity. It is Vishnu, the Preserver of life, whose expansiveness belittles the *Ksheer Sagar* or Milky Ocean that is his domicile. EIGHT is infinite because any outward motion from its point of congruence has a parallel inward motion as well. It represents a constant state of flux - a state of impermanence, as in life.

The Trinity acts as one. Brahma gives the *Guna* or ability to perform. Vishnu gives the *Bhava* or the emotional feeling to perform. It is only the *Shakti* or power given by Shiva that impels motion. And the combination of the three makes GOD.

The body encompassing the "I" or ONE, of EGO or *Ahamkara*, is eventually a zero - empty like a vacuum. A body without ONE or the Ego as its nexus, is *Anant* or endless. It is a manifestation of Vishnu's infinite vastness like the helical structure of DNA that is boundless.

I recognize the Spiritual and the Quantum physical aspects of the number 108. To me they are like life, and that is what this volume is all about.

Parvin D. Syal

Chapter A

BRAHMA

A 15

Aham Brahmasmi

Seated, a child, on His lap
probing wisdom,
atypical for my age
seeking secrets -
where did I come from -
not an inquiry
about my mother's womb
but the womb of humanity
and scrutiny
into entities non-human.
The Big Bang -
Hiranya Garbha -
an outward fulmination
of atoms of existence.
But what caused the bang?
Reality or myth?
Explanations mere tales
over-simplified
for minds simple
explaining concepts complex
not yet set
in concrete,
afloat, pollen seeking
hosts fecund.

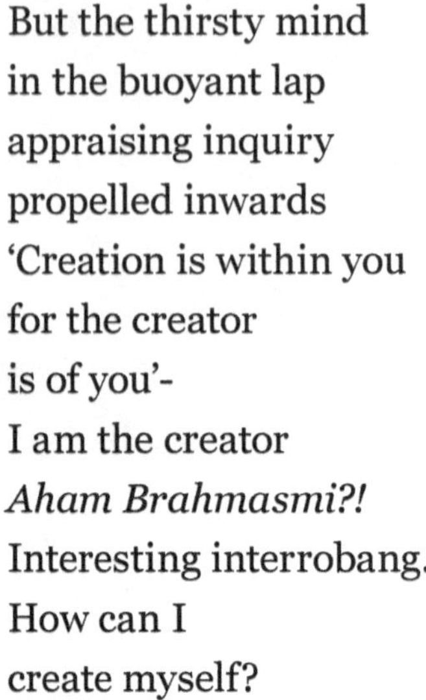

But the thirsty mind
in the buoyant lap
appraising inquiry
propelled inwards
'Creation is within you
for the creator
is of you'-
I am the creator
Aham Brahmasmi?!
Interesting interrobang.
How can I
create myself?

'The reference is not
literal
nor of the flesh.
The *"Aham"* is the "I"
ego motivating
propulsion to counter
any resistance -
the force
behind thought
behind desire
behind need
behind fulfillment
behind gratification'-
thus, says Brahma;
not a wizened sage
with faces pointing
in all directions
seated atop

a lotus
as depicted
in simplistic
calendar art
nor the Brahma
of mythology serialized
for bored housewives.
Brahma, the 1
only 1 capable
of internal combustion
an engine
self-fueled
hurtling towards
future millennia
creating at the will
of a thought
vibration,
of a thought.
vocalized
a cosmic ripple
the static sheet
of tranquility, tweaked
shedding forth atoms
elements elementary
for creation convoluted.
Brahma personified
granting wisdom
as I sit
in His lap.

A 2

Muse #1

I was at the bottom
of a pit vile
desperate and despondent
emotionally desiccated
expression arrested
buffeted by
the tragedy of events
recent.
I was at the bottom
of the pit.

The stage beckoned
to train
vocalize lines
dramatically penned
intoned
at the director's will -
confidence resurgent
discovery anew
eyes focused forward
seeking
and you
in school uniform blue
slumped in the auditorium
taking a break

from the scholastic
matrix of exploration.
My rehearsals
attained meaning
as I felt your aura
my words spoken to you
my theatricality directed
towards you.
Energy dissipated
to envelop
clasp close
a mantle inspiring.

Muse not to amuse
but suffuse
the creativity within.
Find articulation
in words written
and expounded
a garland
painstakingly festooned
petals of words
fragrance of feelings
a circle of love
with no beginning
and no end.

A 3
Creation

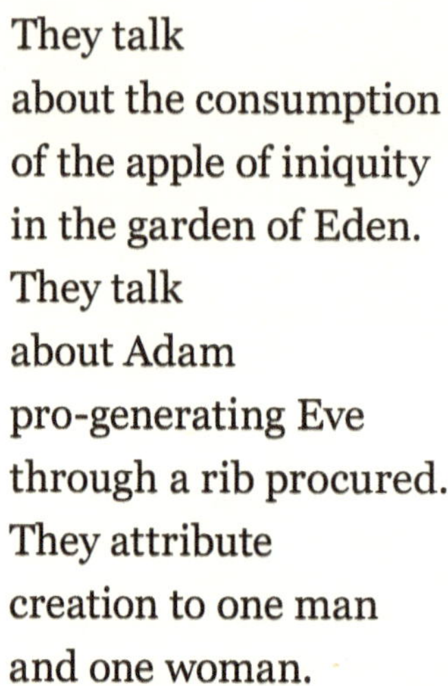

They talk
about the consumption
of the apple of iniquity
in the garden of Eden.
They talk
about Adam
pro-generating Eve
through a rib procured.
They attribute
creation to one man
and one woman.

They talk
about thought and desire
about a word and its vibration
about discordance in space
the elemental congruence
creation of matter
and ensuing life.

They talk
about the Creator
sending forth
his sacred bird
diving into
the ocean primordial

bringing forth
a grain of sand
to create the world
terrestrial.

They talk
about cracking
the cosmic egg
order following chaos -
hiranya garbha -
the womb of fire
flinging forth
florid life.

They talk
the mythologists
conjecture,
philosophers
debate,
anthropologists
narrate
and we still wonder
what really happened,
where we came from.

A 4

A Child Is Born

Barren!
The word spat out
invective vituperative
continually torturing
a woman
denounced and disavowed
for not having
produced a child.
Society medieval
expectations steep
masculine disposition
never suspect
cast to slavish grind
never respected
casual receptacle
for his pleasures.

A rumble of thunder
pursuing
a dagger serrated
renting the skies -
a bolt striking
him
as he lords over
an acquisition fresh.

Burden!
The word spat out
cast out
the master is dead
the family can ill afford
another mouth to feed.

Through the village
a caravan passes
camels laden
heading for
the cross-road of commerce
Samarkand.
A merchant
compassionate
taking her
under his protection
finding her sad smile
a challenge
to convert to laughter,
succeeding
and rewarded justly.
She is with child,
he proclaims
as the city twinkles
on the horizon.

Trading complete,
merchandise laden
homeward journey begun.
Jingling trinkets

conspicuously silenced -
the caravan
breaks its journey;
her erstwhile village
bears witness
as a child is born!

A 5

The Elusive Chord

Four lads
Liverpudlian lads
working class lads
seeking refuge
in teenage dreams -
The desire
to break away
from drudgery,
weekly wages
squandered
on Friday evenings
at the local pub.

Four lads
strumming guitars
banging drums
attempting song
lyrics penned hurriedly
on napkins
futuristic from one
melodious from another
refined
as practice sessions
loom and rhymes mundane
seek rhythm sublime

but as callused finger-tips
caress the strings
discordant chords screech.

Four lads
seeking music
of intonation engaging
not the jingle
of frivolous ditty.
There is a musician
an innovative musician
across the Mersey;
the seeker boards a bus
Birkenhead-bound
fare bummed from Mum
with guitar in tow.
An obliging master
a keen learner
redemption
a sound unique
the elusive chord
destined to spawn greatness.

He'll Follow the Sun
on a Magical Mystery Tour -
Eleanor Rigby and
Lovely Rita will
get back, and wish
Good Day Sunshine
and Let it Be.
Hey Jude, especially

for Julian, as
Someone Knocking on the Door
with Silly Love Songs.
The Band's on the Run.
Yesterday, it was
Penny Lane
forever though
It's a Long and Winding Road.
The journey arduous
Rishikesh eventful
self-doubt quenched
creativity boosted
Maharishi blessed.
Riding into Jaipur
but oratorio bound -
Liverpool once again.

A 6
Guide

A sonorous folk song
the protagonist out of jail
takes a path unknown
rejecting the city
of pain
the love of his life
left behind.
A tale thereafter
of a misguided soul
becoming savior.
Land baked, cracking
under the fire
of a fierce sun.
Taking on a fast
unto death, willing
the gods to relent
nurture the soil anew.
Temptation to flee
resisted.
A duel between
heart and mind
propounding light
over darkness
message clear -
'A pilgrimage site

a place that reminds
of God
a saint a person
whose perception
provokes prayer.
There is no joy
no grief
no pity
no world
no man
no God.
Only me.
Only me.
Only me.'

A 7

Embellishment Of My Life

The falls at Niagara
a stifled roar
as an icy mantle
shackles the river mighty
the ground blanketed
in fresh snow
the winter sun deceptive
temperature near freezing.
The motion of the car
makes you queasy
the heating in the cab
of no help either
the lunch of greasy pizza
and cheese smothered fries
squarely to blame.
Your embarrassment
diplomatically concealed
a memorable meeting
for the first time.

A Christmas day stroll
deserted boardwalk
a still Ferris wheel groaning
the roller coaster
empty threat in the sky

no buskers, no vendors.
A solitary fisherman
throwing a line in
the marina isolated
moored boats bobbing
straining to set sail.

London, your bailiwick
Carnaby Street and Bond Street
Covent Garden and Saville Row
seen through your eyes
shod at Church's
neck-tied at Liberty's
boarding the tube
at Hyde Park Corner
discovering London again.
The treasures in the Tower
the secrets in the Abbey
Churchill slouching
as parliament harangues
the Thames a-bustle
barges on the move,
seeing London through
your eyes.

Boarding the ferry at Harwich
Amsterdam bound - Dam Square
Van Gogh's opus, Rembrandt Square
teeming, coming alive
the Rijksmuseum's oeuvre
tears suppressed at Ann Frank's house

the canals, the windmills
the miniature town - all a blur
concentrated in a few days.

The hover-craft at Dover
Channel crossing to Calais
Parisian evenings, walking
on the South Bank - artists' kiosks,
leaving a lock
at Le Pont des Arts
boats with tourists
frolicking on the Seine,
the sun's rays filtered
through glass stained
dancing on the floor
of Notre Dame.
The Moulin Rouge forbidden
the Eiffel Tower growing on you
the funicular straining uphill
at Sacre de Coeur
Montmartre's frenzied crowds
uninhibited and unfettered
the Louvre - gazing
intently at Mona Lisa
deciphering the elusive smile.

With our daughters in tow,
exploring churches and castles
that there is a surfeit of
but museums are your milieu
the knowledge about art

permeates, energizes, and percolates
as you cultivate
my unrefined sensibilities
and I appreciate
texture and light, the minutiae
of colors blending
the courses of brush strokes
of shifting gaze to
a focal point – as paintings
come alive.

Life, an embellishment
incomplete as
the road still beckons
and we trudge on
ceaseless
in our exploration.

A 8

Bodhgaya

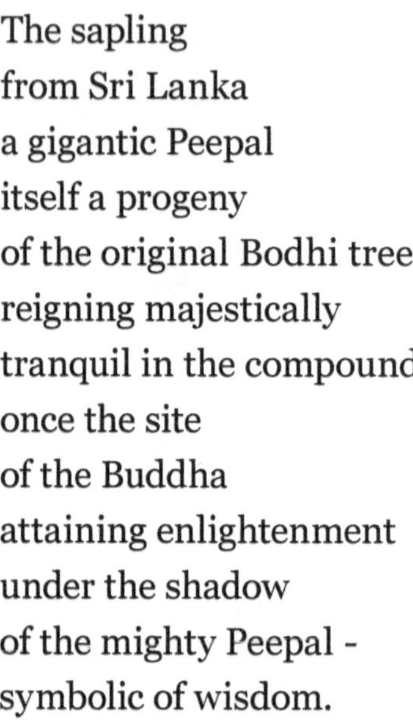

The sapling
from Sri Lanka
a gigantic Peepal
itself a progeny
of the original Bodhi tree
reigning majestically
tranquil in the compound
once the site
of the Buddha
attaining enlightenment
under the shadow
of the mighty Peepal -
symbolic of wisdom.

An afternoon languid
in the post monsoon
coolness of the Indian season;
the River Niranjana
flowing merrily
riding a rickshaw
on the roads of Bodhgaya
campus of
temples dedicated
to the prince
who became

the Light of Asia.
Sitting
under the same tree
eyes closed
transported to centuries past
when Gautam
espoused the tenets
of revolutionary thought:
detachment
as salvation
parables told
koans posed
and issues resolved
as a wave
of humanity
would seek
and be blessed;
guided towards
the path of
attaining Nirvana.

A 9
Muse # 2

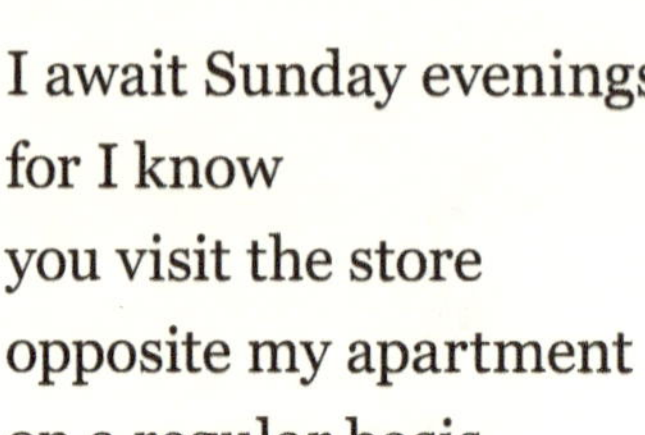

I await Sunday evenings
for I know
you visit the store
opposite my apartment
on a regular basis.

I stand at my window
curtain partly drawn
concealing my presence
inconspicuous
lest you accuse
me of stalking.

I see you drive
into the parking lot
carefully guiding
your sky-blue sedan
into a berth
vacant solely
for you.

You glance habitually
towards my window
and detecting no silhouette -
the room is dark -
walk on nonchalant

oblivious
of my doting gaze.
When and why
did you become
prominent for me?
I know not the answer.
My eyes search for you.
My heart beats for you.
But the chasm
of silence between us
immense.

Time elapses
you haven't yet left.
What is detaining you?
The door-bell rings -
strange
I am not expecting anyone.
My car is not blocking
an entryway.

I walk downstairs
unhurriedly
expecting
some neighborhood kids
and open the door
to find you
standing there.

Time freezes. I freeze.
Your warm smile thaws

with charm and poise
as you extend your hand
seeking permission
to enter my home
and my life.

A 10

Tales From My Father

My father
a child reared
hearing stories
of ancestral wealth
yet sustained
ironically at the mercy
of others.
His mother widowed
helpless and forlorn
charting the course
for her two sons
one still at breast.

Formative years
of privation and deprivation
forgotten, left behind,
migrating across the ocean
in search of a life better.
Pioneers in a land
virgin and fertile.

The iron snake
winding its way
across the plains
and highlands,
settlements springing

along its course
place of sweet water,
Nairobi,
a city born.

Among compatriots
imported by the colonial masters
a night clerk's job temporary
monitoring the operation
of the iron horses.
Ambition unfettered
the drive of adolescence
a desire
to sever the cord
and sail
to the great white nation
and study law
restrained, held back
by fraternal exaction.
Forays
diverse stints
settling as
a legal aide
white Scot sahib a mentor,
a Parsee attorney, benefactor
a career launched
knowledge self-garnered
studying under
a dangling light bulb
labor rewarded
dividends earned
lessons passed on.

Tales
illuminating
of adventure related,
of being trapped
in a herd of elephants
dispersed
by setting
the savannah on fire -
legal files up in smoke.
Tales
of nights
doused in a tank
of icy water
anti-pyretic to prevent
black-water fever.
Tales
of sacrificed self interest
saving erring kin
from the moving
wheels of justice
to win for another day.
Tales
of adventure
and spirit pioneering
carving progress
pushing the limit
a raw body politic
polished
into a diamond
radiant.

The lap
of a doting father
soon a lap of luxury
forged by efforts Herculean
and patience
spread across
decades.

A 11
Exodus

Britain needed
to connect the port
at Mombasa
with the inland
Bugandan kingdom
in the Protectorate
of Uganda.

Britain needed
labor to lay
lanes of steel
over rugged terrain
mosquito infested
and domain
of lions wild at Tsavo
and through
the Rift Valley
lacerating the land.
Workers inducted
in India
with promises
of adventure
and riches beyond
ripe for the picking.

Britain needed
to administer
lands East African
acquired by
the European elite
in its scramble
for Africa.
Ergo,
the Indian literati
artisans and tradesmen
lured with a future secure
in a frontier land.

Britain needed
a buffer community
to rule over
the population native
so, naturalized
the Asian emigres
as subjects of Britain
granting passports
blessed by
the Majesty Britannic.

Britain needed
to flee the colonies -
the clamor
for independence
bore fruit;
the white colonists
compensated

resettled in England
the rest left to their fate.

Britain needed
to distance itself
from subjects foreign
so, threw roadblocks
regulations restricting
entry into Britain
unless white.
Duncan Sandys
Commonwealth Secretary
disbanding the empire
rejected proposals
for immigration
to Guyana
introducing instead
vouchers for the subjects
to start anew
in the Isles British.

Britain needed
time to enact
the proposal biased
but before it became
the law of the land
an Asian tsunami
holding papers Britannic
jammed British ports;
the exodus from Kenya
had started.

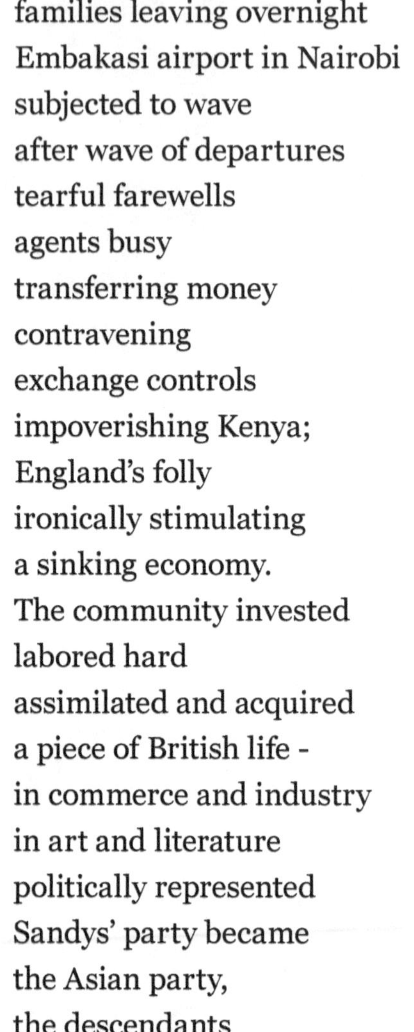

Planes were chartered
families leaving overnight
Embakasi airport in Nairobi
subjected to wave
after wave of departures
tearful farewells
agents busy
transferring money
contravening
exchange controls
impoverishing Kenya;
England's folly
ironically stimulating
a sinking economy.
The community invested
labored hard
assimilated and acquired
a piece of British life -
in commerce and industry
in art and literature
politically represented
Sandys' party became
the Asian party,
the descendants
of the exodus masses
became mayors and ministers
and occupied
#11 Downing Street.

A 12
Pokhran

A desolate spot
in the desert
observed by foreign
eyes in the sky
defiant symbol
reliance native
pride national
soaring
when the country
conducted a test
nuclear.
Branded an aggressor
Though practicing restraint
keeping dormant
combative ambition.

But the borders
remained pervious
tensions abiding
enemies salivating
teeth gnashing
eager to bite
had to be blunted
malintent foiled.

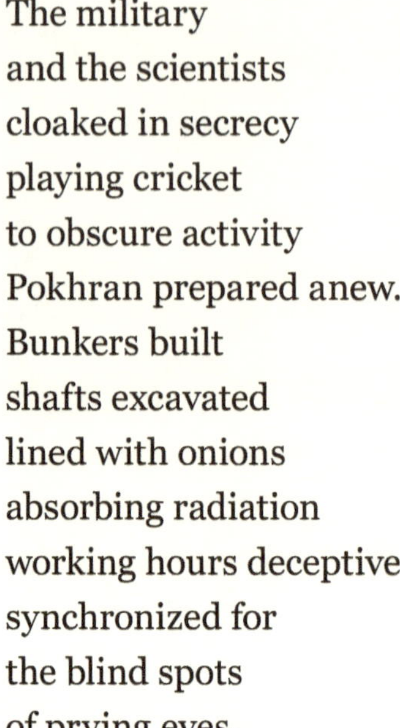

The military
and the scientists
cloaked in secrecy
playing cricket
to obscure activity
Pokhran prepared anew.
Bunkers built
shafts excavated
lined with onions
absorbing radiation
working hours deceptive
synchronized for
the blind spots
of prying eyes.

Operation Shakti
yielded three tests
the country gate-crashed
the awe inspiring
club of the elite.
A deterrent it stays
but vigilance eternal
walking softly
carrying a big stick.

A 13
Inauguration

Excitement abuzz
the gold embellished card
arrived in the mail -
a VIP invitation to
the President's inauguration.
Having toiled for months
on a campaign arduous
the fruits of labor
ripe now for plucking.
Washington DC thrilled
in excitement hyperbolic
the nation's representatives
packing venues varied
in pre-inauguration delight.
Tours of the Capitol arranged
Congressmen as docents
commemorative pictures
in the well of the House
feted by the state's senators
in the Hart Building.
Obligatory visit to Arlington
respects paid to leaders departed
homage paid to the founders
of the Republic -

Mount Vernon
picturesque and majestic.

Morning of the special day
cold and bleak
all roads leading
to the Mall
thousands staking
positions of vantage.
Ushered by volunteer staff
seated, looking up
the seat of government
pomp and glory on display
amid tradition
the parades of dignitaries
before the swearing-in
the address by
President Clinton
applauded and cheered
by a partisan crowd
awaiting an end
to policies destructive.

Tuxedos and gowns
ball-room anticipating
celebrity spotting
Elizabeth Taylor resplendent
Barbara Streisand elusive
Whoopi Goldberg the girl next-door.
The power-couple
Hillary and Bill

on the stage exuberant
greeting with smiles
Tipper and Al to follow
to thunderous applause.

The dawn
of a new era
returning home
having partaken
of an event
historical.

A 14
Mother's Lap

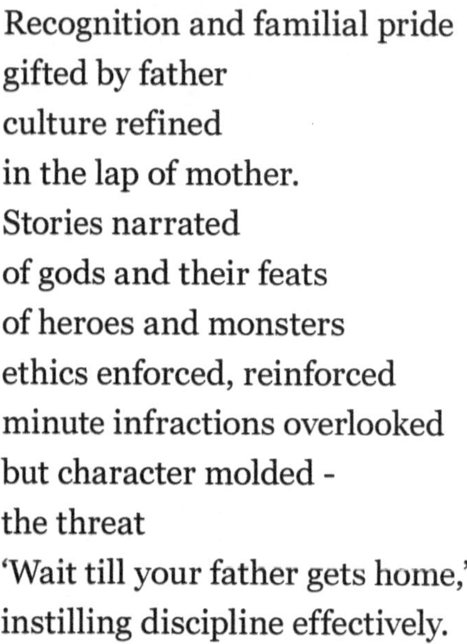

Recognition and familial pride
gifted by father
culture refined
in the lap of mother.
Stories narrated
of gods and their feats
of heroes and monsters
ethics enforced, reinforced
minute infractions overlooked
but character molded -
the threat
'Wait till your father gets home,'
instilling discipline effectively.

Overseeing the completion
of school assignments
monitoring the time spent
with neighborhood kids
ensuring that playmates
didn't exert influence corrupting.

A friend gave me
a pencil at school -
Mother made me return it -
fierce pride of self.
My friend had cigarette butts

in his pocket, and it was I
facing the inquisition
though innocent
of any such breach.
The iron fist a necessity
keeping one on track -
to paint the canvas
of susceptible life
with colors creative
not splotches of
disorder cataclysmic.

She aged majestically
Mother
angelic as ever
mirthfully smiling
mannerisms idiosyncratic
teasing playfully
recollected pleasantly.
Blissful visits
to the temple together
the blessings she bestowed
as I paid obeisance
in the morning
the tranquility she exuded
reciting passages
from the Ramayana.
I could not see her halo
but felt the radiance
she perpetuated.
She is gone

but the benediction remains.
She is gone
but the cradle's teachings
remain to guide
through the travails
of time.

A 15
Shadow

Living in my own shadow
an umbra of ignorance
oblivious of events
transpiring behind
my back
poked at, prodded,
and stabbed
pushed into a morass
of my own creation
the tarry inkiness
of my own shadow.

A pivotal point exists
recognized only
when rigidity relents
into moments malleable
tensile strength trapped
flowing into a mien positive.
A turn on the axis
all that is needed
to leave my shadow behind
staring straight
into the eye of the sun
dazzled by the light bright
and the specks of negativity

float away into oblivion -
my eyes adjust
and I see bathed
by the sun
the golden path
to my future
leaving the shadow
of ignorance behind.

A 16

Messages To My Daughters

I
THE ROAD LESSS TRAVELLED
(with apologies to Robert Frost)

The road less travelled
unique, especially
when a high road,
affording opportunity,
motivating adventure,
introspection, and growth.
A pad appropriate
to launch the spirit
into heights soaring
gliding on a breeze gentle
alongside clouds soft,
cohorting with eagles majestic,
eyes sharp and keen
surveying the landscape
flourishing below,
swaying with the movement
of wind-rippled fields
harmonious
in tune
with music divine.

The road less travelled
yours to explore
carve a course
for yourself
fulfill needs
attain desires
hone skills
as the hand divine
sculpts malleable clay
with a spatula giant
shaping the path
as you dictate.

The road less travelled
is designed for you.
Carpe diem
seize the moment
for now, it is your time
now your opportunity
now it is your road.

II

EDUCATION - EXPRESSION OF EVOLUTION

Seated on an arena chair
anticipating
commencement
post education
expression
of evolution.

What words to articulate
what wisdom to convey
realizing
knowledge is imparted
wisdom inborn
looks can
be embellished
beauty inborn
tales garnished
fact just one
craft learnt
talent inborn.

Axioms to adopt -
you can just act
or act justly,
better to adjudicate
than be judgmental,
better practical
than mired
in premises
unproven.

Look outwards
but seek within
eyes open for vision
but closed in meditation
to be visionary.
Profit from a prophet
not be a prophet
for profit.
Learn to trust

then be entrusted.
Walk tall, head aloft
feet grounded in reality
experience the small acorn
then delight
in a forest oaken.
Soar high in plain sight
only the afraid
fly under the radar.
Speak softly
words
not just bulky
but bearing heft
random thoughts
create poetry
unfettered
unlike words prosaic.

Tell your story
not just gab
but first listen
persevere and excel
seek ecstasy
and enlightenment,
Sat Chita Ananda
Nirvana,
in the beating
rhythm of the heart.

And remember
better a joker
than a joke,

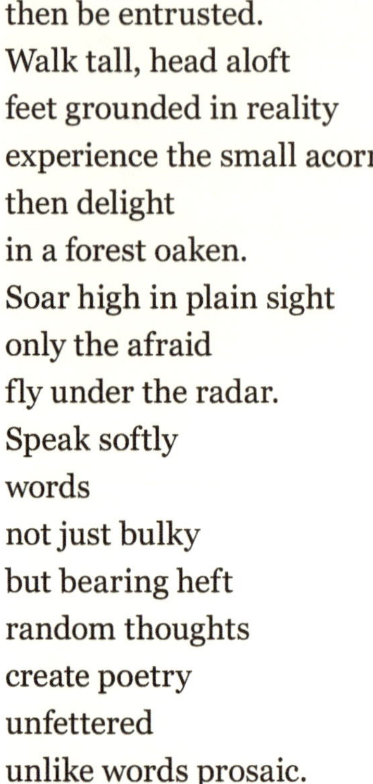

better a strip of cloth
than stripped of cloth,
better a rich mind
than opulence empty. ,

And forget not
that one crosses
the road to get
to the other side.

III
MONOCHROME VERSUS EKTACHROME

Curves and bends sharp,
upswings and descents,
occasional zig-zags,
contours elliptical -
life is not about
straight lines alone.

Triangles and rhomboids,
cones, crescents, cubes,
and circles concentric -
life is packaged not just,
in boxes insular.

Beams of moonlight,
dancing on a shimmering lake,
sunlight undulating on
a Saharan dune,
refractions and reflections,
deflections and mirages,

all form life,
not just a wave
monochromatic.

Life is not about
black and white -
mostly shades of gray -
and when starting afresh
a slate blank,
awaiting dyes fresh,
not necessarily
within the confines
of tracer lines,
but audaciously
seeking frontiers new.

So, the lilacs and the mauves,
saffrons and antimonies,
teals and turquoise,
fiery reds and crimsons seductive.
sky blues and Irish greens,
sunset ochres and
mustard yellows,
all await your creativity
on the palette of life.
Go ahead
pick up your brushes,
don your aprons,
and paint your life,
to your heart's content
on this canvas wide.

A 17
Dev Saab

The set in a Bombay studio
shooting a scene
with Sulochana as your mother
courteous and convivial
between takes
conversation animated
about Prem Pujari
your debut directorial.
I had walked into the studios
a fan, I left
as your friend.

Years of separation
contact scant
continents apart
meeting again destined,
Des Pardes premiere,
Los Angeles bonding
eternal.

Your legendary status
never minimized
cultivated charm disarming
public appearances zealous
open and receptive
warm smiles omniscient

no transgressions by scowls
or words unpleasant
recognizing adulation
that places you
on a pinnacle of acclaim.

Established as a member
of my family
letting down your film persona
relaxed napping on the sofa
watching the news
or quietly contemplating
listening to my daughter
at her piano practice.
Standing in the kitchen
evening meal being prepared
requesting favorite dishes
relishing the presentation
on the dining table.

Standing in the foyer
of a Vegas casino
in moments of frustration
shouting at each other
hugging moments later
in mutual synchronicity.

Celebrating milestones
traveling across the country
exploring places new
scouting talent fresh

for your venture next.
Relaxing in a NY hotel
walking to Times Square
imbibing the place unique
ideas for the movie next
germinating and gelling.

In the non-obtrusive privacy
of personal space
discussing matters of the heart
learning you viewed me,
'a son
a brother
a friend close.'
Advising
on decisions about life
supportive
in times of need
jubilant I named
in your honor
my daughter
new-born.

On road trips
Grand Canyon and
the parks of California
stopping at locales
of cinematic interest
listening to *ghazals*
Farida Khanum inspiring.

Sitting on the carpet
at the Nav-Ketan penthouse
music sessions with creators
of hits melodious
regaling with tales
of a career long
and moments memorable.
That cruel day in December
your passing sudden
tributes and tears
services in London
pressing the button
with your son and nephew
ashes
your earthly existence
but the soul immortal
as are you
through your films
and ever a part
of my being.

A 18
Poet Laureate

Gitanjali
translated into English
fails to capture
the soul
of Tagore's
magnum opus.
The poet's
native Bengali
caresses the landscape
kisses the waters
of the Ganges
and delves deep
into the mind
of the man common.
I read it not in Bengali -
Hindi, a close second -
and visualize
the setting
for the words
of the sagely savant.

Dare I emulate
string words into melody?
Dare I emulate
spin stories of

suppressed sparkle
and liberation eccentric?
Dare I emulate
stage productions
of kingly courts and
courtyards communal?

Inspiration on a roll
efforts to emulate
failure at the outset.
None can be
the complete cache
of creativity
endowed
in the white maned
wizard of words -
Tagore.

A 19

Silver Mane

He walks in
silver mane
gelled in place
waxed mustache
in a regal loop
belt undone
Rolex placed
on the desk
ready for a weigh-in.
Polite pleasantries
disposed
the fortnightly discourse
commences in earnest
topics random
predicated on mood
or the topicality
of time -
from ornithology
to oenology
from customs Jewish
to Hindu rites.
Singapore adventures
Australian outback trekking
Roman recess
discussed with

equal relish
in detail minute
immensity of knowledge
profuse.
Study of waves
pattern of currents
velocity of winds
magnetic effects
of changing poles.
Operas and concerts
services in the temple
politics at the Reagan
dissected in a manner fine.
Expanding my knowledge
trivia filed away
for conversation later.
I look forward
to visit with
the New Jersey professor
retired on the west coast
following his passion
playing with switches
and rail-road tracks
laid in his back yard
in recollection
of his father-
a proud railway-man.

A 20

Muse #3

The bus ride
is long and bumpy
the diesel engine
droning noisily
the chatter
of excited students
indistinct.
But my eyes
only for you
as you sit
in the back row
your head recumbent
on his supporting
shoulder.

Picnicking group
the Iveti Hills
adventurous trek
through Wakambaland
rocky hills
streams gurgling
on their pebbly descent.
But my eyes
only for you
as you giggle

girlishly
your hand on his shoulder.

The campus
back again
dropped off
the students' dorms
heading for respite
narrow beds
in cramped rooms.
But my eyes
only for you
as you walk
with his arms
around your shoulders.

What,
what do I have to be
for you to glance
in my direction?
What,
what do I have to do
for you
to be aware
of my presence?

A 21

Paddy's Wigwam

There were days
when I needed
to ruminate
withdraw into my cocoon
communicate with
the feelings within -
I needed my space!

The urban scene
always a disincentive
for an exercise such
the parks, too public
my room, too confining.
I find myself enticed
by the Liverpool Metropolitan -
the Catholic Cathedral -
Paddy's Wigwam in local slang,
to provide a few hours
of hushed solitude
undisturbed and un-noticed
I sit in one of the pews
eyes closed
though cognizant
of the surroundings
channeling my energies

inwards
to chart and correct
life's courses.

Unconventional cathedral
boomerang trusses
flying buttresses
a truncated cone
with a towering
crown of pinnacles
symbolically rising
an adornment of thorns
pain immense
taken upon himself
to provide salvation
assuage sins
savior of his followers.
The faithful
light candles
kneeling in prayers
seeking communion
and having
been blessed
returning
to the mundane.

Rejuvenated
finding anchor
the pivot and gyroscope
of life in sync
I leave

to visit another day
on my journey
of exploring
my self.

A 22
The Pandit From Nairobi

A fledgling community
in a land foreign
congregating
to practice their faith
in halls rented.
Rituals and prayers
elders conducted
devoid of guidance
of a well-versed *pandit*.

Funds raised
land sought
a church converted
into a temple
to attract the devoted.
Committees formed
applications sought
petitions filed
suitable candidate
sponsored
to lead the flock -
his credentials solid;
he had served in Nairobi.

The *pandit* walked in;
middle aged

clad in traditional garb
salt and pepper hair
combed neatly
horn-rimmed glasses
scholarly demeanor
smile disarming
scriptures imbibed
impeccably.
His interpretation
cognizant of the times
his manner simple
of imparting knowledge
to the unversed.
His discourse wide
inter-faith convocations
soon convened -
San Diego, San Francisco
Sacramento and
far flung Florida too.
The *pandit* carved
a following,
a name for himself
and for those
starved of guidance
his steadying hand
a God-send
in time of need.

A 23
The Guru

The country was susceptible
its youth without direction
the meaningless war
in far off Nam, numbing.
Hitler's threat
had been neutralized,
Enola Gay's mission
established US supremacy
but the country was susceptible -
its youth without direction,
the Abrahamic faiths
a balm no more.
The psychedelic effects
of Acid and the opiates
a Lewis Carrol burrow
into eerie nightmares.
Flower power waning
frustration the bane
the whole country ploughed
for the seeds
of new ideas
exploration afresh
a scrutiny of the self
before an outward gaze.

The Guru stepped in

offering compost
for a field malnourished.
A yogi learned
in the intricacies
of stimulated sensuality
serendipity sublime.
His message magnetized
he created a branch new
of a faith ancient
the learning of an idiom new
explaining experience eclectic.
An imposing figure
clad in white robe
pious yet practical
probing paths approaching
progress personal.
Ventured into vending
clout political
attained positions
in fora international
and the followers
a force
spiritually inclined.
No more
cannabis craziness
to corrupt
the people,
no more
debauchery
to demonize
the people.

A 24
The Crush

Miles and decades
removed
from the country
of our birth,
sauntering on a bluff
overlooking the Pacific
on a warm
breezy summer evening
reminiscing of
lives in another time -
how you grew up
in a community
of Railways employees
camaraderie among families
bonded by service
to an organization common.
How siblings shared space
and resources scant.
How you found
your niche
endowed with
thirst for knowledge
complementing
smartness inborn;
a leading candidate
for scholastic enterprise.

As an educator
in training,
you recalled quite well
that you taught
my class and
remembered me
as a normal pre-teen -
shy nor exhibitionist
in manner,
apprehensive and withdrawn
at moments,
preened for attention
at times other.
Perhaps
it was physiology
but most likely
your attractive personality,
that attracted
me towards you -
a childish crush
whose memory
stayed a part of me.

We walk now as friends,
in the company of our spouses
and you are
now aware that
you brought a blush
to my cheeks once
and made
my heart
flutter once.

A 25
Machakos Memories

The school mandates
a term of community medicine
experience in the field
at the Machakos campus.
Days spent
inoculating children
educating mothers
trudging through *shambas*
taking a census
tabulating illnesses,
and discussing results
yawning and tired
in post-dinner clusters.
Awaiting another day
another drive by jeep
another village
another set of subjects
more inoculations
more data collected.

An evening discourse
a school full of children
pubescent giggling
birds and bees explained;
folks in the villages

disbelieving graphics
of mosquitoes magnified
mocking the charts
illustrating
the anatomy complex
of a pest pernicious -
but the cool ambiance,
bucolic pulchritude,
hilly terrain at dusk
scenic,
the comradeship
of colleagues bonding
etching moments
memorable.

Early morning walks
in the campus fields
cherry tomatoes ripe
green peas in the pod
sweet
French beans snapped
crisp and refreshing
whistling tunes random
greeting the day
with the vigor of youth.

A break from studies
a free rein
of the hostel kitchen
baking short-bread
plum jam to garnish

and singing songs
whiling the time away.

Sojourn into town
a swim in the
clubhouse pool
chairs relaxing
on manicured lawns
sipping tomato-juice
while shooting
the breeze.

The schedule means
a week-end duty
of covering
the hospital clinic
with my partner
assisting
the emergency room -
a kind registrar
letting us off early.
Welcome entertainment
the only cinema
in town
playing old classics.
Why does the *bui-bui* clad
Fawzia
from the Swahili community
show an interest in me?
Why don't I reciprocate?
I don't know.

Perhaps I am too focused
on the future
to notice the present
as it unfolds.
Perhaps,
I am dubious
of the moments evolving
doubtful
unwilling to be side-tracked -
inaction an escape
an excuse
for my own
nonchalance.

I wish I had
known Fawzia better.

A 26

Tattoos

Skin art
self-expression
or a fad?
My mother
had her name
on her fore-arm;
my father
an *OM* on his hand -
tattooed tags
of identification.
Now a fascination
to burnish one's identity
in an age of memes
pictures and emotags
denoting emotions of life.
Adults struggling
with the concept;
mothers vocalizing
apprehensions,
fathers shrugging off
an inconvenience,
more frustration
than indifference.
Would I be lucky
to escape this incursion?
Heavens no!

I did not, however
shrug this off;
sketched the concept
on art paper
a lotus and
the symbol of *OM,*
accompanied my teenager
to the tattoo parlor
as the artist
inked her back
in colors bright.
The foxes
and the musical notes
that were added
were of independent
volition.

The second child
met resistance
futile arguments debunked
determined to emblazon
her favorite design
on her fore-arm.
In all fairness
the artist applied
the image of
the Oscar trophy
in all its golden glory
and gave the child
a conversation-piece
forever.

A 27

Corechella

Magnet schools
creating programs
unique
acronyms denoting
specialties
targeting
the heart
of the matter –
core curriculum
core values
core goals
aphorisms galore -
all work and no play
heading for dullness -
ergo, a celebration
of music
ala Coachella
of the California desert.

Corechella
designated . . . The festival;
student bands
vying for a spot
competing for trophies,
and our daughter

crooning away
practicing in the shower
belting notes I thought
were beyond her range.
Come the important evening
we join others
on the floor
a mad frenzy
of structured noise -
cannot but help
scream and cheer
the debut performance
of our award winning
star.

A 28
Shani Shingnapur

I used to dream
of colors
that would coat
my imagination
an amalgam of
running rivulets
coalescing to form
a mellow mauve
a lilting lilac
a propitious purple
luminescence akin
a peacock's pride,
a violet plumage
of shades
unfamiliar to me.

Shani Shingnapur
pilgrimage devoted
to Saturn.
An ebon monolith
rising majestic
unfettered, unroofed
proud protuberance
that bled

when first prodded.
A self-evolved deity
Shani
present through millennia
venerated with
ritual worship
pouring of oil
to coat and caress
the rock charcoal black.
Freshly bathed,
having cleansed myself
adorned in a *dhoti*
white
prayer platter in hand
marigolds to offer
and oil to daub
I await my turn
in a line
of devotees.

I rub the oil
on the deity's symbolic slab
and notice the emergence
of my puritanical purple
my luxuriant lilac
my mellifluous mauve
the hues of my dreams
swirling under my finger-tips.

The stone speaks to me
in a language
of color
and having received
the message
I levitate
into the future.

A 29

Ganga Descending

A visit to India
incomplete
without a trip
to Haridwar
at the foot-hills
of the Shivalik Himalayas -
the gateway for Ganga
as it descends
onto the plains.

The railhead at Saharanpur
convenient for the journey
carriage boarded
in sweltering heat
sandwiched between pilgrims
seeking salvation
with a dip
in the holy river.

The mass of humanity
hurrying towards Har Ki Pauri
an expanse of marble
chequered black and white
and slippery steps
leading into the river.
Chains bolted

into the concrete
support
preventing devotees
being swept away.
The cool water
sweet succor welcome
on a hot summer day.

A leisurely walk
the bazaar hugging the river
religious paraphernalia
trays of confectionary fresh
the sights and smells
of pickled mangoes
mounds of spices -
ocher vermillion
in hues vibrant
baskets of marigolds
garlands strung
flowers fragrant
gemstones and *malas*
of rare *rudraksha*
all enticing the pilgrims.

The evening prayers
not only devotion
on display
but display
a devotion
hundreds of *diyas*
a flotilla on the river

seeking salvation
of their own.
Evening wafts of air
refreshing
feet dipping in the water,
a repast simple
served on a leaf platter
hot tea sipped
from quaint *kasoras*
earthen taste enriching
animating the senses,
enlightenment
not only spiritual.

Blessed
heading back
on the midnight train -
Saharanpur awaits
again.

A 30
Ajaccio – Corsica

The calm waters
of the Mediterranean,
an ocean in training,
tranquil - the liner
sails into Ajaccio
Napoleon Bonaparte's
native capital
of Corsica
vassal to France, yet
fiercely independent
marching to the tune
of its own drummer
tolerating throngs
tourists sampling
cuisine local,
trudging, cobblestones,
long queues
to scan casually
Napoleon's extravagance.
But I seek
the hills
Alpine heights
narrow winding roads
quaint villages
lamenting the loss

of sons
to the lure
of urban wealth.
Vegetation diverse
nurturing the bees
producing honey
distinct
sweet, light amber -
elixir of the hills
dark, tinged with bitterness
product of the foot-hills
a complement to liquor -
medicinal gift from the gods.
Ambrosia
accumulated pollen
stow-away on the legs
of the worker bees
a force to sustain
generation
and rejuvenation
of the forests
Alpine.

A 31
New Age Pilgrims

The plains of Salisbury
ordinary and non-imposing
till the dramatic rise
of a circle of rocky monoliths
some connected
horizontal trestles
ancient – mystical origin
magnetic in appeal
the artifacts of Stonehenge
drawing me closer
on a mid-summer dawn.
I feel the vibration
my *chakras* activated
the aura of collective
Druid invocation
a coven praying
in a circle
holding hands;
a desire to meditate
in the lotus position
worldly eyes closed
third eye perceptive
envisaging the scene.
Stonehenge - an altar
Stonehenge - a medium
of an enlightened mind.

Onward journey - Somerset
Glastonbury - new age magnet
for neo-pagan persuasion
kneeling at the graveside
where King Arthur's bones lie
ruins of an abbey
walls populated with tales
of an age of chivalry
and chicanery.
Climbing the Tor
symbolically masculine,
drinking deep
at the Chalice well
divinely feminine
nature's communion
like Shiva and Shakti -
provision of life sustained.

Northern coast of Cornwall
sprawling ruins of Tintagel Castle
on the hill - Arthur's domain
Tintagel, the setting
for the legend
of Tristan and Isolde
looming over waves battering
the rocky cliffs and
visible over the sea line
the cave of Merlin
guiding wizard
of Arthur's court.

Sites ancient
beliefs ancient
legends ancient
new-age pursuits
of ancient emblems
comprise a pilgrimage
for today.

A 32

The Float

Aesthetic, altruistic, amenable
attending to the pinning
of petals, and gluing
of seeds, to adorn
the artistic float
entry for Pasadena's pride,
The New Year's Rose Parade.

Arrayed in a row
with platforms other
in a warehouse gigantic
near the Rose Bowl
the float has volunteers
decorating images vivid
imaginatively carved
meticulously spatulated.
The flowers delicate
wilting when compared
to the freshness
of your manner
and the fragrance
of your being.
I find courage
approach and introduce
with hands folded in greeting

as you dazzle a smile,
acquaint yourself
and present
your husband delightful.
Thus, begins a
friendship common
lasting the decades
that ensue.

A 33
The Olympics

Prognosticators of doom
envisaged a city
gnarled in traffic
freeways seized
frustrated drivers
turning to anarchy.
But Los Angeles
in the summer of '84
an exemplary city
smooth through
the Olympic games.

Opening ceremonies
Coliseum awash in anticipation
friendly competition on display
athletes jostling through
the Olympic Village
at the USC campus.
Special passes
enabling access
as we host squads
from the home country.

Cheering teams favorite
field hockey on astroturf
screaming fans goaded

by celebrities in attendance.
Providing local insight
commentators in the sky-box
broadcasting to the homeland.

Driving to Chino
Arcadian Prado Park
sprawling site for
shooting matches;
hair trigger pistols
targeted clay pigeons
thrilling for the trained eye
of fire-arm
aficionados.

The closing ceremonies
of pomp and roaring approval;
a city proud in success
a new model of games
to emulate in the future.

A 34

The Rise Of The Phoenix

When winds swept the plains
when floods uprooted trunks of trees
when thunder bolts mangled the skies
when upheavals saw the migration
of populations dispossessed
the homeland was lost . . .
Seeds atop the steeds of time
branches grafted and transplanted
grounded continents apart.
Each one of us
left our square yard
of personal space
but carried a bushel
of memories
of traditions
of friendships
of associations
of aspirations.

Beckoned by foreign shores
saplings cultivated
oft-times brutalized
but sheltered -
familial sheaths of protection
nurtured and then abloom

a plethora of color and fragrance
a rainbow of benevolence
a desire to embrace again
that square yard of space.

As our pods ripen
seeds are launched aloft
to seek if destined
the soil of origin.
A gathering of collective energy
pooled goals and resources
and out of the ashes
of fires once spent
we rise
a phoenix
eyes set once again
on the homeland -
an integral part
of our collective psyche.

A 35
Muse # 4

Broken hearted
in despair
rejected by the one
I thought was mine.
A walk through
your portal
welcoming
the mellowness
of your spirit
the sweet nectar
of your speech
ambrosia remedial.
Broken spirited
I lay my head
on your shoulder
and you ran
your gentle fingers
through my hair
evoking memories
of mother remote
and wiped tears
from my grubby cheeks
to restore resolve;
healed my ego
jolted and jilted

revived steel
to my spine
as I reclaimed
my worth
and walked out
tall again.

A 36
Tridevi

The three facets
of the Godhead
Brahma, Vishnu and Shiva
delegated to create
maintain and regenerate
are themselves incomplete
for any force of energy
wasted without
a receptacle to rein in
their dispensation
into a steady stream
nurturing
humanity starved.

Brahma
the keeper of the tomes
of knowledge
abetted by the Goddess
Devi Saraswati
depicted with a *veena*
benefactor of music
knowledge and wisdom;
the river concealed
enriching Yamuna

and Ganga at
their confluence.

The universe sustained
Vishnu on the serpent
of time
manifestation of
marching moments
acquisition of
desires fulfilled
attributes of
the Mother Goddess
Lakshmi -
the one who
facilitates attaining goals
of wealth and prosperity
the gifts of Bhu Devi -
Mother Earth.

Shiva
Mahesh, Rudra, Bhairon
mendicant unhabituated
tied to nobility
of responsibility,
married to Sati
Parvati, Kali, Gauri
Durga - names varied
attributes and aspects
one
mother to Ganesha
Kartikeya and Ashoksundari

and sibling of Vishnu.
The pantheon of Gods
abbreviated
without the Tridevi -
the three consort.

Chapter B

SHIVA

B 1
Shiva

Shiva,
spine and axis
of the universe
self-created
the one with no end
nor beginning
of no parentage
no lineage to proclaim.

Shiva
that which is
and is not
the light of day
and the inky darkness
of night.

Shiva
purveyor of peace
rejuvenating
and redesigning
founding the images
of his worship
Jyotirlingas springing
at sites diverse
from the heart
of the Himalayas

to coastal communes
each with attributes unique
and sagas related
in texts ancient.

Shivalingas
adorned ritualistically
crowned with *bael* leaf
dressed in sandal paste
bathed in milk dripping
as mantras are recited.

Shiva
as Nataraja
the lord of
Tandava
the dance of destruction
reconstruction
into life renewed.

Shiva
as Rudra and Bhairon
irate destroyers
of evil and ignorance.

Shiva,
Neel Kantha -
the blue throated one
who swallowed
and arrested
in his gullet

the poisons,
toxic output
of the ocean
when churned.

Shiva
the mendicant
with matted hair,
covered in ash
riding his mount
the bull Nandi
on the avenues
of Kashi
to claim in marriage
the hand of Parvati
daughter of the mountain,
manifestation of nature,
uniting with Shiva
for balance cosmic.

Shiva
the lord of Mount Kailash
celestial abode
stabilizing pole
of the planet.

Shiva,
father of Ganesha,
the remover of obstacles
grantor of boons
fulfilling desires

to rid the self
of egos binding
and overpower
the shadows of ignorance.

B 2

Death Of A Leader

The whimpering demise
of the lionized leader
death creeping in
hemiparesis struck
slinking away
into the pages of history.
A parade funereal
galvanized gun-carriage grand
trudging along
the Jan Path -
the People's Road -
towards the pyre
on the banks
of the Yamuna.
Rising flames
proclaim a dynasty
and his words -
citations of mid-night trysts
beamed incessantly
on the airwaves;
Frost's woods
dark and deep
immortalized

lines doodled
left behind
on the desk
of the departed leader.

They commemorate
his demise;
of reputation too
an unkind history
unraveling the shallowness
of his character
filing away the veneer
of demeanor suave
his legacy
the vivisection of the nation
his folly
denying the nation
a spot on the world stage
his polity
tattered as neighbors vile
gnaw at borders fragile.
Ladakh still vulnerable
Nathu La tense
Doclam volatile,
vituperative
challenged progeny
over-indulged
by wealth misbegotten.

They commemorate
the demise
of the leader
but there are
no more tears
for the fallen man.

B 3

My Guitar Gently Weeps

The transmogrification
gradual
search for meaning
onerous
strumming in vain
fame premature
screaming fans
no longer pumping
energy at a nadir.
Rejuvenation
an elixir
along the Ganges
leaving behind
a Guitar
Weeping Gently
angst of forlorn love
empty life
vacuous and incomplete.

Here Comes the Sun
the Guru
directing exploration
inwards
illuminating
attaining

the Sweet Lord
Krishna Hare Krishna
chants purifying
aurifying the experience
a dip in the Ganges
at Rishikesh.

Learning
the complexities
of *ragas*
the *sitar*
to master
strings weeping
different chords
mirth of random playing
laughter
incense sticks
and stimulants
of nature -
Shiva's gift to humans.

Returning westwards
Dark Horse
subjugating territory new
creating sounds
not heard before
an approach
to music new
from the Cavern
to dens of intensity
new philosophy

new discovery
new expression
feeling
new.

B 4

Muse # 5

I should have known
that you lived
in a world of fantasy
populating unrealistic
notions of romance
addling your mind.
You thought
yourself
a fragile
porcelain doll
to be handled
gingerly at all times,
your complexion guarded
by a perpetual straw hat.
Nimbly holding
my supporting arm
painting always
the image of
susceptibility
felled
by any disturbance mild.
Your domestic views
hinged
on impractical demands -
a princess craving

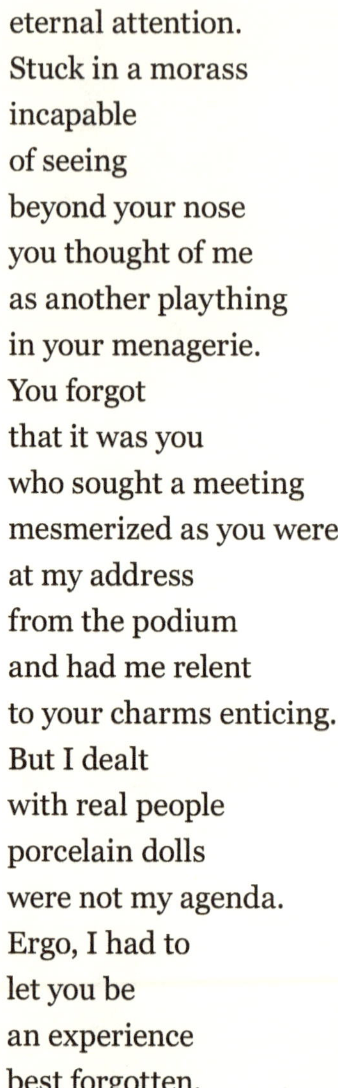

eternal attention.
Stuck in a morass
incapable
of seeing
beyond your nose
you thought of me
as another plaything
in your menagerie.
You forgot
that it was you
who sought a meeting
mesmerized as you were
at my address
from the podium
and had me relent
to your charms enticing.
But I dealt
with real people
porcelain dolls
were not my agenda.
Ergo, I had to
let you be
an experience
best forgotten.

B 5
Square Dancing

Right angled triangles
have certain proclivities
Pythagoras postulated -
square dancing
on the hypotenuse
being the same sum
as squares waltzing
on the other two sides.

Triangles that are congruent
side, side, side,
and side, angle, side,
drummed in and practiced
as angles watch
the sides proving
egalitarianism.

Squares boring
inclined rhombi
parallelograms
and rectangles
whirring and whirling
Oxford compass sets
attempting to create
figures exact -
angles reassigned

calculating values
unassigned.

Circles and arcs
spoked to the center
the value of pi
Aryabhata ordained
circumferences cycling
areas calculated
radii impaled
in techniques fragile.

Matriculate to the level next
spatial thinking
sines and cosines
trigonometric functions
defined by ancient masters
tangents to confuse further
secants and cosecants
to torture anew
a fledgling mind
untrained to think in
dimensions three.

The dance with Maths
more a salsa volatile
than a waltz mellow -
crunching numbers
deriving relations
solving equations
and progress

to such an extent
that log tables
are of antiquity;
Casio calculators rescue
a free-fall
to the bottom-line
calculations completed
more a magic
of the fingers
than a trained mind.

B 6

Professor Emeritus - E.T
Baker-Bates

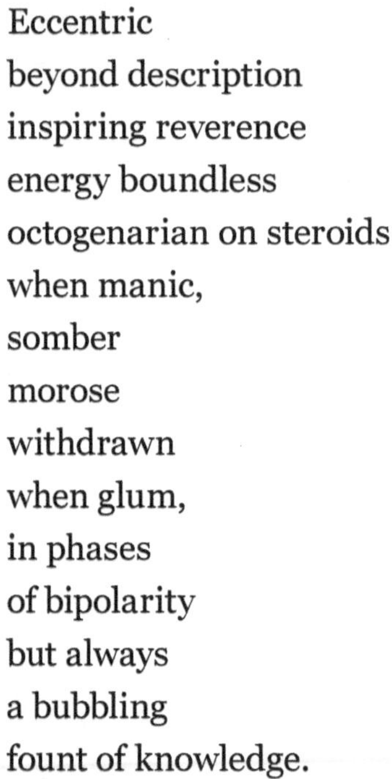

Eccentric
beyond description
inspiring reverence
energy boundless
octogenarian on steroids
when manic,
somber
morose
withdrawn
when glum,
in phases
of bipolarity
but always
a bubbling
fount of knowledge.

An apparition
like Gandhi
clad in a white
linen sheet
doing his medical rounds
in a sleeping ward
at 2 in the morning
with me

the resident intern
sleepily
tugging along.

Standing
at the foot of the bed
diagnosing scurvy
and Buerger's Disease
by merely touching
a limb algid -
such clinical acumen
passed forth by diffusion.
A father-figure
taking under his wing
a neophyte raw
passing knowledge
shaping compassion
creating a physician
to be a healer
complete.

His lonely journey
from affluent Liverpool's
Rodney Street
to the town of his birth,
Lancashire coal mining
surpassed by Pilkington Glass
alone and lonely
seeking affection
from gratifying residents
catering his soup de jour

a ménage of left-over meals
to an unsuspecting group,
escaping
for being a vegetarian.
But Eccles cakes
and fresh mince pies
strawberries and cream
a welcome sight.
Sharing cucumber
and tomato sandwiches
between patients
in the afternoon clinics.
Patients seeking serenity
someone to talk to
are farmed off to me
a willing recipient
of punishment logorrheic.

I have to leave
for pastures green
and am given the gift
of knowledge ensconced
in the very fiber
of my being
carrying a slice
of B.B. with me.

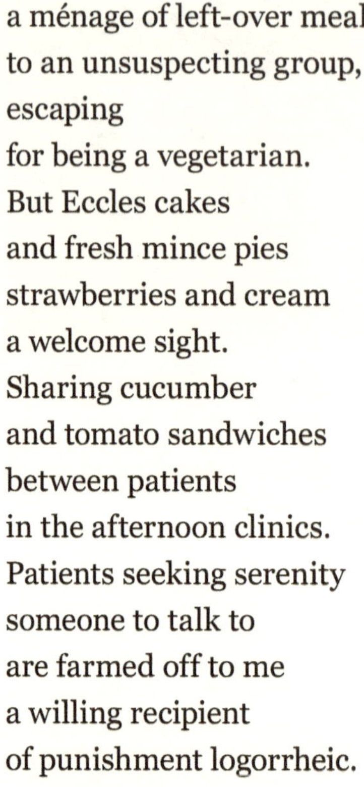

B 7

Pestilence

Lepers
castigated by society
cast into colonies
disfigured and purulent
infected and infectious
living hell on earth.
Saints walk among them
giving solace and succor.
Some profess
the healing touch,
miracles more talked about
than witnessed.

Time passes
the microbe
understood
the antidote
developed
the disease
arrested
and pestilence
a piece
of the past.

But are we geared
to face
new lepers
new progenitors
of disease maleficent?

B 8
Mau Mau

Displaced from their villages
arable land appropriated
kipandes issued
concentration camps
wired with barbs
screams for mercy
daily beatings
all to justify
colonial policy
lording over the Gikuyu.

Driven underground;
the Aberdares
forests of
the Mau Hills.
birth of a rebellion
fight for freedom
preservation versus privation
dignity versus desecration
branded as thugs
accused of murder and rape
terrorizing colonials
on stolen land
yielding blood crops -
sacrifice

of the labor native.

Mau Mau
a name frightening
bogeyman casting
a pall of panic
in places urban.
Homes broken into
robberies rampant
grain and cooking oil
mainly targeted
rations to feed
the rebels
beleaguered.
Neighborhoods
self-policed
armed with scout whistles
and steel-tipped *rungus*
miscreants to deter.

Mau Mau
cultivating fear
brown man's conundrum
whom to slight,
whom to fight?
Pangas, razor sharp
weapons wicked
home-made pistols lethal.

Mau Mau
scourge for
the settlers white
hunted
and an innocent population
left behind
made to pay
retribution for the sins
of the men absent.

A line drawn
in the red soil
as years
of guerrilla tactics
bring the colonials
to heel
and ships sail
Europe-bound again.

My land
my golden harvest
mine once more.
My nation's flag flutters
my nation's anthem
tribute to those
whose blood
wrought freedom.

B 9

The Scout Master

Wooden crates
painted red
loops of rope
for handles
locked
lying strewn
on the classroom floor
gray and somber
akin the mood
in the school.

The Scout Master
drowned
in an attempt valiant
to save a young boy,
swept in the river
caught in a whirlpool
squelching life away.

Bodies recovered
funerals hurried,
sadness a cloud
as students struggle
to understand
the tragedy

confronting
budding minds.

Tears rolling
down my cheeks
stifling sobs
in my soiled sleeve
sleep elusive
disturbing thoughts
replaying in a loop
sighs uncontrollable
Why? Why? Why?

My father rests
his calming hand
on my brow
guides me to
the water tap
helps refresh
a wasted face.
He sits with me
on the edge of my bed,
'The soul does not die,'
he intones
as Krishna did to Arjuna,
'The soul cannot
be drowned nor burnt
for the soul
is immortal;
the body impermanent
like clothes

adorned by the soul
cast aside
at the time of death
as it moves on
to be born anew.
Mourn
the loss of a body
rejoice the release
of the soul
as it seeks
to merge
with the creator.
Salvation and moksha
the goal
an end to
birth after another birth.'

Calm descends over me.
I don't understand all
that my father explains
but his tone is angelic
his words soothing
his touch comforting
and the span
of his knowledge
expansive.

I am no longer a child.
I've taken my first steps
towards adolescence.

B 10
Truant

Parochial school
prayers and
songs religious
starting the day
institutionalized values
moral and ethical
should have imbued
but a young mind
audacious
itching to break rules
explore what is
on the dark side.
Intellect ill-defined
discrimination
a concept uncharted
the whole
lemming-like
blindly following.
So, it was with me.
A friend inciting
to cut classes
and chase a wild ride
on the city's buses
aimlessly traversing
remote roads.

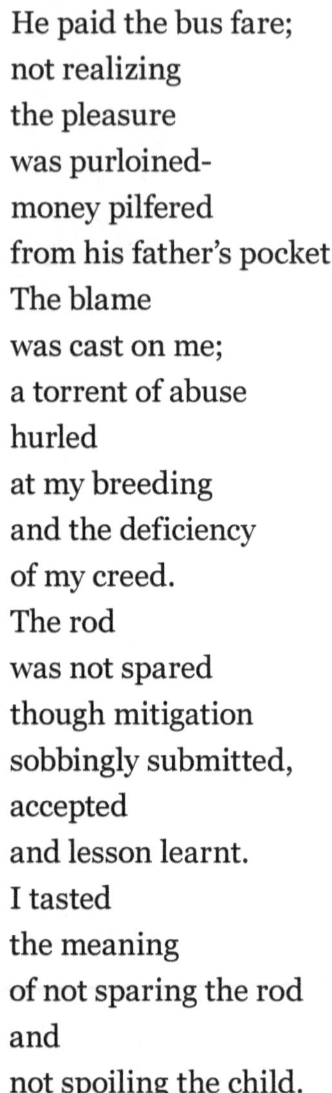

He paid the bus fare;
not realizing
the pleasure
was purloined-
money pilfered
from his father's pocket.
The blame
was cast on me;
a torrent of abuse
hurled
at my breeding
and the deficiency
of my creed.
The rod
was not spared
though mitigation
sobbingly submitted,
accepted
and lesson learnt.
I tasted
the meaning
of not sparing the rod
and
not spoiling the child.

B 11

Assassinations Political

I

Frail
leaning on the shoulders
of aides devoted
attending his last
prayer meeting
disturbed
dastardly destruction
wrought by a country divided
limbs amputated
trainloads of corpses
a theocracy created
and a voice gentle
no longer effective
lonely in the wilderness
amid ambition political
supplanting
interest national.
Bapu
confronted a bullet
the name of Rama
on his lips
blood staining
white cloth

crumbling
like virtue
in his land.

II

The grassy knoll
a limousine grand
road curving - wide
the popular leader
Dallas crowds
waving, fawning -
a sound of gunfire
life drained
doting wife helpless.
An end
of dynamism
of hope
of propelling a nation
forward -
an end of
vanguard of the world.
Who was the enemy?
Who the assailant?
An execution or retribution?
Political intrigue?
Mysteries of unanswered
questions buried alongside
at Arlington.

III

My people
black people
scions of slaves
forcibly foisted
on fields fecund
picking cotton
toiling on plantations
dotting the south.
My people
equal in the eyes of God
segregated
beaten
chained
discriminated against -
set them free.
My people
part of the commons.
My message
Gandhian.
My quest
Christian.
Seeking respect
gunned down
as I stand
on the balcony
of a motel
in Memphis.

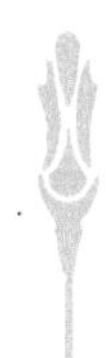

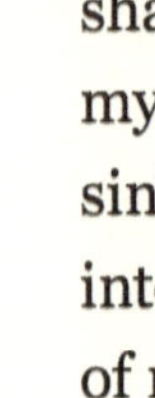

My dream
shattered
my people
sink further
into the morass
of racial inequity.

IV

Footsteps to follow
complete
a brother's agenda
heal a nation
divided by race and class
dreams to realize
both Jack's and Martin's
and others
who dared to ask.
The glory of an evening
victorious
short-lived,
an assassin lone
at close range.
The Grove
shrouded in grief,
doctors at Good Samaritan
unable to save his life.
The Kennedy legacy
sheared.
Bobby is gone!
Bobby won't be president!

Bobby
a lion among men
leaving
what-ifs behind.

V

Africa was chained
its land usurped
nations sliced and served
ravenous predators
from across the seas.
Kenya was chained
its land usurped
White Highlands
snatched by the colonials
natives banished
villages nibbled
cultures denigrated
the deviously devout
peddling a system
foreign.
The whisper for freedom
growling
growing into a roar
and *Uhuru* at last.
The rise
of a leader mature
charming, disarming
probably a threat
to the ruling chiefs

mowed down
on a limp Saturday noon
as he, Tom Mboya,
walked out of a chemist's.
Lament Africa
for a new brand of leadership
is assassinated
in its prime.

B 12
Rodney Riots

A little black girl
short by two pennies
walking out of
a convenience-store
with a carton
of orange juice
shot for theft
by a Korean owner.
Anger pent up
waiting for the magma
to blow.

A black motorist
Rodney King
driving erratically
pulled over
mercilessly beaten
racist cops
stomping and kicking
in xenophobic rage
unplugged.

A white jury
in a red-neck town
acquitted
those who breached

honorable conduct.
A spark was lit
the genie
out of the bottle
as protests turned ugly.

An unfortunate driver,
malfunctioning truck
dragged out and beaten.
Black power misplaced
misdirected arson and loot.
An inflammatory mayor,
Police Chief draconian
the faculty of discernment
distressed-
my city burnt.

Korean snipers
positioned on roof-tops
the white folks
afraid to leave home
the gangs black -
the Crips and Bloods -
terrorized my city
expressing rage rightful
in a manner wrong.

Appeals
formations of commissions
clergy at the podium
community workers

pounding pavements
finally contain
the Molotov is capped.
A rancid return
to numbed normalcy
my city scarred
a new name
carved
into the urban lexicon
of Los Angeles.

B 13

Massacre Of 1984

Making a martyr
of a common goon
exploited religion
a tinder-box.
Misguided and stubborn
a leader basking
in self-perceived glory
committing a litany
of follies
gunned down.
Retribution, exacting revenge
cleansing the city
of a community
peaceful and industrious -
South Extension
Maharani Bagh
other sections
of Delhi barricaded.
Marauding gangs
Trilokpuri and Sultanpuri
across the Yamuna
and cities across
the nation -

in genocidal madness
seeking to let blood
inflicting a people
gone insane.

'I cannot stand by
and watch my neighbor
butchered.
I cannot stand by
and see necklaces
of tires set aflame
to snuff out
screaming life.
Stop this fanatic mania.'

A chain of
responsible citizens
linking arms to protect
our brethren targeted.

The wails of the widows
the whimpers of the orphans
still crying out
seeking justice
the guilty under the aegis
of those in power
need to be flushed out
and pay for the atrocities
they instigated -

not the scapegoats
nor the sacrificial lambs
offered as the token guilty
but the ones who ordered
the massacre -
setting brother against brother.

B 14

Strawberry Fields Forever

The image
round Gandhi glasses
eyes twinkling
merriment and mischief
deep
piercing
seeking
lilting lyrics
rhythm
songs to enrich
poetry reflecting
an age confused
in search of meaning
wars futile
politics of self-gratification.
Lennon evocative
Strawberry Fields provocative
Imagine
I am a Dreamer
reigning anthem.
Lucy in the Sky
with Diamonds
promising.
Alice in Wonderland
reinvented,
I am a Walrus,

tom-foolery
begets moments serious
Instant Karma
cyclical life
Watching the Wheels
Go Round and Round.
Woman,
an ode to Yoko,
affectionate
possessive
obstreperous
inspiring too -
Starting Over
Give Peace a Chance
disrupted.
A forty-year-old
gunned down
in a New York street.
Millions of candles lit
homage
tears flowing
an artiste slain
mid-stream.
And all
that is left
is a guitar
on a stand
and those round glasses
atop a white piano-
his memorial
the Imagine Room
in Liverpool.

B 15

Ted Heath's England

The country
cannot afford
to provide electricity -
the miners
are on strike.
The work week
trimmed to three days,
TV off at 9.00 p.m.
traffic lights dysfunctional,
staggered supply
of power -
there is
a shortage of fuel.

Cold,
miserably cold
awaiting the train
at Sale station
spot jumping
to keep warm
on the frigid platform;
the waiting-room
an icebox
pathetic
like the Prime Minister

Ted Heath
failing
to move
the country forward.

The train
anemic in its approach
lumbers to a stop,
the warm seat
in a welcome coach
an answer to a prayer -
wish the journey
was longer -
not just a hop
to St. Helens Junction
where hopefully
the bus would be
on time.

Cold
wretchedly cold
the winter of '73
with political downfall
policies of failure
privileges removed
as the coiled-up masses
ready to spring
out of control
not to be neglected
anymore.

B 16
I.R.A.

Referred to
euphemistically
as the troubles
the Irish divide
with roots
entrenched deep.
Sectarian differences
a religion
misinterpreted
Catholic pitched
against Protestant.
The northern counties
defiant towards
the south
ferociously royalist
defining the course
of the Irish
on both sides
of the border.

The thorn
in the side
polluting and pernicious
inciting revolution
insurrection

taking the fight
to foreign soil.

I run out
of the mall
with my aunt
in tow.
Sleepy suburban Lewisham
in the spotlight
I.R.A. bomb
albeit diffused
in the store.
Others
less fortunate -
conflagration
acrid smoke
craters in the roads
shrapnel embedded
buildings limping
maimed bodies
death.
The perpetrators
sewer rats
disperse
to council estates
bland and bleak
to plan more
for another day.

St. Patrick's Day celebrations
at the Irish Center,
127 Mount Pleasant,
Liverpool -
bomb threats
desert streets
amputate revelry -
rushing back
in coaches
homeward bound.

Futile?!
Not for the
Irish Republican Army
nor the Sinn Fein,
not for the ones
incarcerated
in the E Block
at Portlaoise Prison.
They draw attention
to their cause.

The sewer rats
exterminated
peace again
on the streets
of London.

B 17

Muse # 6

Autumn trees bare
skeletal fingers clawing
at skies bleak
gray and foggy
damp cold suspended.
An apt location
a tryst
in the deserted park
breaking the news
that England no longer
holds the sway -
you are bound
for foreign shores
and warmer climes
to exploit
opportunities new
to advance
your career forward.

No, there are
no tears
no imploring
just a lump
in my throat and
heaviness of heart

as I gaze
into your eyes
for the last time
imprinting the memory
of our being
a unit
once.

A final hug
the wall between us
already erected
an awkward feeling
unfamiliar
as I turn around
and walk away
sure
that you have
done the same.

A ray of sun
struggling to breach
a passage
through the mist.
There is still hope
that light will abide.

B 18
The Dragon

Soldiers ill prepared
lost in terrain untamed
mountains unkind
guarding a border
porous and pervious.
Inept leader dormant
the seething dragon
stirring into action
aggression against
a proclaimed friend
now declared foe
a quest for expansion
of land and ideology.
Benign no more
a red wave
to subjugate
hegemony over
a force passive.

Heroes are born
in theaters of conflict -
a bulwark against
the onslaught
braking intent
nefarious
the laying down of life
for the motherland.

Nation wakened,
a primordial scream
heard at the border
mobilized to defend
arrest the advance
towards the plains.
Death and martyrdom
not worthless
the dragon blunted
despite the loss
of Aksai Chin
in the Ladakh
wilderness
and the defilement
of Arunachal.

Talks upon talks
inconclusive
evil intent checked
but not contained.
The 1962 debacle
of Nehruvian ineptitude
festering still
the menace
of military might
the sword
of Democles
dangling over
the body politic.

B 19

Flight From Jammu

The State
is in a state
of siege
the winter capital
Jammu tense
with movement
restricted
heightened security
for terror grips
the border
and the enemy
within
infiltrated from
a neighbor malevolent.

We have to leave;
Delhi awaits
to launch
further ports
in a schedule
intense.
We have to leave.
The flight from Srinagar
delayed
hours creeping by

waiting at the airport.
No flights after 5 p.m.
the Air Force has
restrictions in force
for purposes defensive.
Helpless
pacing up and down.
4.35 p.m.
P.A.S. announcement
departing passengers
directed to line up
near the runway.
As the arriving aircraft
taxis to a stop
passengers alight
from the front
as we board from
the rear of the plane
and airborne
at 4.55 p.m.
The State's Chief Minister
who is on board
caused
the initial delay -
I look out and spot
an Air Force escort.

Time for a nap.

B 20

Mumbai Mayhem

It was a dastardly November
the city of Mumbai assaulted -
assassins landing
launched from
a neighbor bellicose
to spread mayhem
and destruction wanton;
an attack on society civil.
Terror preached
a nation's weapon
of distorted values
religious edict
shanghaied.

The monumental icon
Taj on the Bay
apneustic
choking on smoke acrid
fires raging within.
The city
fights back
as slumbering leaders
dither
and heroes emerge
through valor personal.

The front desk manager
wounded but returning
to flush out
the cowardly roaches
who maimed
and killed sadistically.

A lull returns
to a city shocked
lurking insentient
for weeks to come.

The *maidan* deserted,
the Gateway of India
with nary a soul
the road barricaded
leading to the Taj -
I stand a lone figure
dwarfed
by Shivaji's statue
behind me,
ruminating
digesting the events
of the few days past
and marvel
at a city
vibrant once more
undaunted and undefeated.

B 21
MLK

King
a messenger of peace
religious instruction
and decent mien
influenced by
principles Gandhian
prompting
disobedience civil.
The march at Selma
address at the Mall,
Washington D.C.
a sea of pliable faces
watched hawk-like
by Edgar Hoover's minions.
How dare
a black man
rise to such stature?

Confederate mentality persists
the South segregationist
apartheid
under another label.
Gunned down
in Memphis
living on

a legend
celebrated
in Atlanta -
a mausoleum serene.
I stand there
in remembrance
tears trickling
emotion clouding
my mind
failing to understand
one's hatred for another.
And later, when I link arms
with his widow, Coretta
to sing
We Shall Overcome
I feel part
of the movement
seeking equality for all.

B 22

White Man's Burden

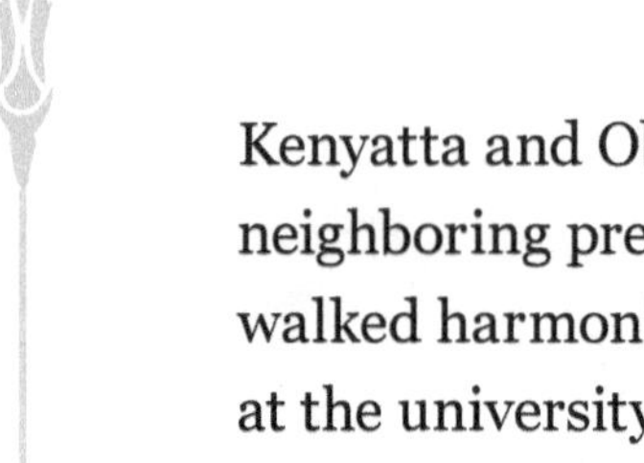

Kenyatta and Obote
neighboring presidents
walked harmoniously
at the university convocation
proclaiming amity fraternal.
Obote banished
by a coup d'état
replaced as ruler
by the army despot,
Idi Amin Dada,
a boor uncouth, rotund
terrorizing people
to retain power.

Attracted to the widow
of an Indian industrialist,
incensed at her refusal,
and secret escape
from Uganda,
the dictator
self-proclaimed
savior of Africa
signed an executive order
banishing from the nation
all people South-Asian

regardless of citizenship -
deported
leaving all assets behind.
Stateless people
refugees accepted
by Canada and Britain
leaving behind
an economy collapsed
and a state failed.

Practicing shenanigans buffoonish
urged his white sycophants
to carry him shoulder high
proclaiming suzerainty
over former colonial powers.
A devout Muslim
providing sanctuary
to EL AL hijackers,
attaining notoriety
on the world stage
jolted and shaken
by Israel's military action
whisking the hostages away
from under his nose.

Evil ends one day
and his day came too.
Exiled to Saudi
died an inglorious
death
syphilis riddled

condemned
by history
and the curses
of his victims.

B 23
The Show

The idol from Mumbai
singing sensation
ruling the air-waves
slated for a concert -
the auditorium
will be packed.
Announcements are made
a local orchestra
to augment
visiting musicians,
the selling of tickets
frenzied.

The show
starts late
people ambling in
oblivious of the time
chattering congregation
in the theater's foyer
disregarding flickering lights
signal to take
their seats.
The opening act
is ready.
The star of the show

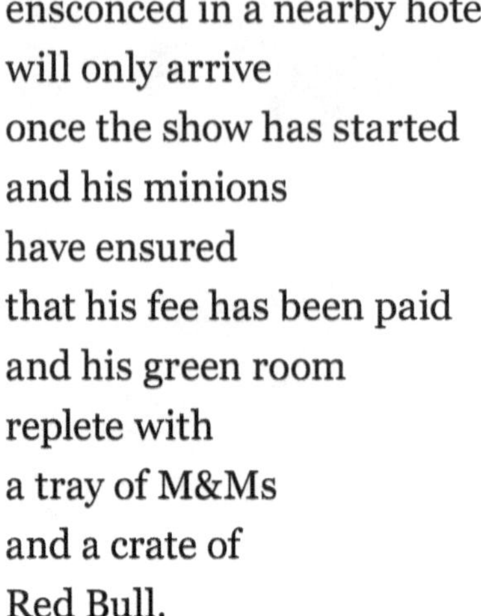

ensconced in a nearby hotel
will only arrive
once the show has started
and his minions
have ensured
that his fee has been paid
and his green room
replete with
a tray of M&Ms
and a crate of
Red Bull.

The patience
of the audience
taxed
as the organizers
hog the mike
basking in their
fifteen minutes of fame
earned by
forsaking thousands
in the enterprise
of entertainment
star-struck
by the celebrities
from abroad.

Select patrons
have been promised
photo-ops
with the star

who balks
at the prospect.
Cajoled and persuaded
to pose for a few
promoters prodded
guaranteed future gigs.

The cycle continues
only the artiste changes
egos are satisfied
bragging rights maintained.

B 24

Muse # 7

Leaving a note
under the wipers
of my car
arranging to meet
for the 10.30 break,
driving with me
to the Hurlingham Arcade
for a cream soda
refreshing red
ice-cold Schweppes
and talk about
your experiences
as a physiotherapist
and mine
as a doctor
in training.

Your hometown
on the coast
meant you lived
in a hostel
away from the family
independent and progressive.
An occasional evening out
masala chips at Exotica

the extent
of our involvement.

The missive
under the wipers strange
a whole letter
in a government envelope.
I read it in silence
singularly disturbed
that you won't
share that beverage
with me anymore
as our innocent
recess rendezvous
a subject of gossip
and your potential
radiologist fiancé
took umbrage
at the trysts.

I spot you
in the corridors
of the hospital
but walk away
closing
behind me
another chapter
of fickle life.

B 25

Crying In The Chapel

The monthly movie moment
always special in school
the auditorium crowded
waiting eagerly
for an Elvis musical -
Jail House Rock
or Blue Hawaii
Fun in Acapulco,
Kid Galahad -
romantic fantasies
for young minds
craving the music
a rage world-wide.
An exchange of tidbits
gleaned from fan-mags
and picture cards
a collector's milieu.

The hip-swiveling
pelvic thrusts
mirthfully regaling
squealing fans
but condemned
from the pulpit.
The Afro-centric

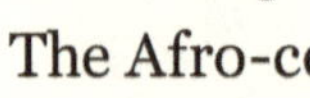

bent in the music -
the King labeled
a renegade
but as popularity
thrived, influence grew
Elvis a legend
crooning sweet romance -
Are You Lonesome Tonight?
Imploring quick response
It's Now or Never!
Themes foreign
locales foreign
instruments foreign
Marguerita with mariachi
ukuleles in Blue Hawaii.
The voice always
captivating
the soothing solace
of tears of joy
Crying in the Chapel
Amazing Grace
reaching new heights -
Southern roots anchored
old values never die.

B 26

London March

I was roped into it;
a march in London
followed by a rally
in Hyde Park
to protest terminations
of pregnancies.
My belief that women
had the right to choose
opt for what
was good for them . . .
I was roped into it.

I was sweet
on one of the nurses
I worked with
her Catholic values
notwithstanding,
incentivized for
the coach-ride
to London,
despite the
absurd hypocrisy –
in my mind,
a mockery
of the march.

Zealous groups
vociferous groups
indignant groups
from over Britain
snaked their way
into London town,
and marched
in order of slots
defined town by town
ward by ward
parish by parish
in an exercise martial
but in demeanor
like a fiesta.

Yes,
there were mocking protestors
lining the route
placards highly visible
threats not so visible
but invective and jeers
deafening any noble intent.
Marching with
a devoted lot
I reflected
on my beliefs -
'Was I right
in what I thought?'
Partially so
'It was for a woman
to choose

what happened
to her body
but only
on advice medical.'
Yes
it was right to abort
in cases of incest
or rape,
to save
a mother's life;
other reasons
probably suspect.

The tiny embryo
scaffolded by
a skeleton of cartilage,
a connective rete
of neurons primitive,
sustained
a heart pumping
the elixir of life
through capillaries fragile.
Life indeed
voiceless
defenseless
needing the protection
of an organized march

I was a changed man
on the ride back -
long highway

egressing London
tired eyes
involuntarily closing
and she -
her head on my shoulder
satisfied
that I had gone
with her,
roped in
though I was.

B 27
Egotistical Rand

Adolescence
approaching adulthood
marching to the tune
of idealism puerile
spirit rebellious
mind fertile
receptive to
thoughts revolutionary.
Non-conformity
damming eons
of peaceful flow
repository to ideas
destabilize order
authority of any ilk.

Atlas Shrugged
John Galt becomes
a role-model
The Fountainhead
Howard Roark
self-made genius.
Ayn Rand
cult figure
indoctrinating feelings
against fascism

and communism
fostering movement
Libertarian
eventually doomed
to be a slave
of the Ego,
serving only
the proud in the self,
individualism sans
consciousness social.
Rejected
through realization
that society
makes the man
and not man
worshipping
himself
in a temple
of self-glorification.

B 28

The Seat Of Power

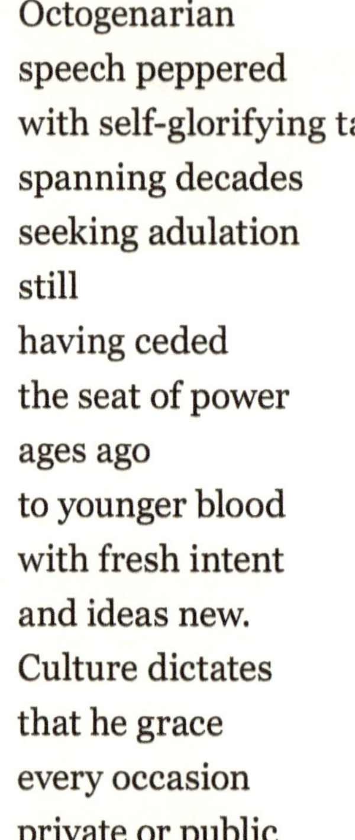

Octogenarian
speech peppered
with self-glorifying tales
spanning decades
seeking adulation
still
having ceded
the seat of power
ages ago
to younger blood
with fresh intent
and ideas new.
Culture dictates
that he grace
every occasion
private or public
mike in hand
relating oft-heard
anecdotes forgotten
to relevance.

The limousine awaits
sycophants
seeing him off
making sure

the camera records
their presence
and then converging
for a snide dissection
of his rambling words
voicing
that he now retires
to enjoy the pastures
of his abundance
acquired through
position of
favor political.
The hunger
for power unabated
the thirst
for praise unquenched
the desire
to seek news coverage
incessant.
The one-eyed reigns
over the realm
of the blind.

B 29
Conflagration

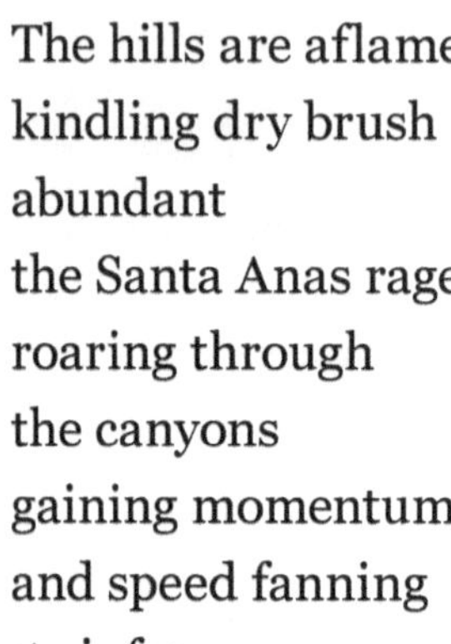

The hills are aflame
kindling dry brush
abundant
the Santa Anas rage
roaring through
the canyons
gaining momentum
and speed fanning
an inferno
in their wake.

Sirens blaring
fire engines racing
to thrash
the annual curse
of the season.
Amber flames
on steeds of gusts fierce
jousting with each other
leaping and dancing
licking grassy kindle
devouring all
in their way.

Surges of wind
transport embers

devices tiny
effective as napalm
carpet bombing
stray spaces
threatening abodes.
Hoses employed
walls watered down,
roofs saturated
drying in a jiffy
the heat catastrophic
as the fire jumps
the highway.
The traffic gnarled
anxious humanity
streaming the news
and Waze apps
on mobile devices
seeking
the quickest
route out.

The sky black
choking smoke
floating ash
cinders jousting with
eaves exposed -
the hills a conflagration
too close for comfort.
I pack my essentials
medications and mementos
computer devices,

into my car
and join the exodus
fleeing the environ.

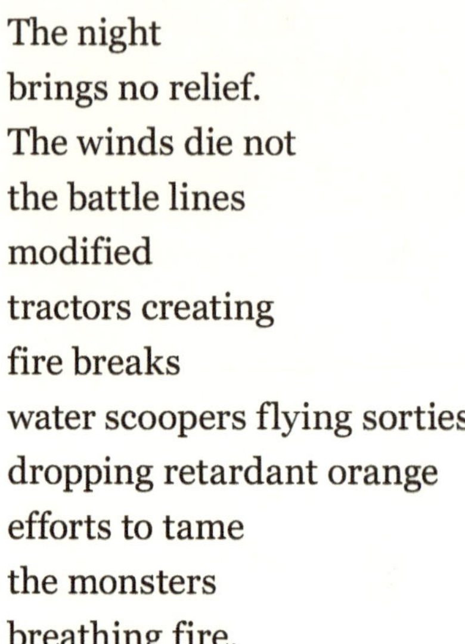

The night
brings no relief.
The winds die not
the battle lines
modified
tractors creating
fire breaks
water scoopers flying sorties
dropping retardant orange
efforts to tame
the monsters
breathing fire.

I am glued
to the news
follow the locations
of areas affected
relieved
my street
has escaped
the blaze
raging through
my town.

B 30

The Guitarist From Guatemala

The clinic open
frequented often
by the same patients -
Mexican and El Salvadoran
from Honduras,
Guatemala, Columbia
and faraway shores
Chile and Argentina -
visiting week after week
more for social discourse
than needs medical.

A unique culture
alien to my sensibilities
being a product staid
of wainscoted offices
politely private
and singularly terse.
The receptionist
shouting in vain -
the clinic
a village-market
noisy and discordant.

The octogenarian
native of Guatemala

a mariachi band singer
in a former life
brings out his guitar
serenades the patients
with songs amorous
much to my growing
annoyance as I try
to auscultate living hearts.

The manager,
sweet Latina from Honduras
soothing and calming
explains, the singer
is lonely, craving attention
that he got before.
Patience a virtue
annoyance in abeyance,
adopting demeanor pleasant
treating all
with a smile
discounting
disturbance mild.

His smile guilty;
he's aware of his
infraction of the norm,
but my greetings
polite and genuine
ministering to maladies
of body and mind.

B 31
Muse # 8

There was a spat
between us
we disagreed
on issues wide
the juncture
of our lives
disparate
tugged at
by forces contrary.
Interests best
served by
ways separate;
the T junction
a sign of
divergent finality.

Consequences unexpected
alienation
from common friends
memories
hounding
delegated
to be forgotten –
a task conscious.

I had thought
you were a painful
episode of a gullible past
when emotion ruled
logic did not prevail.
I was still unschooled
unsophisticated
and ignorant
in the ways
of the world.
A simple knock
on the door opened
in polite response
resulted in widening
the chasm
between us.

There was a spat
between us;
it could have been
worked out
through discourse polite
and
the launching
of our lives
into different
spheres of space
could have
been avoided.

B 32

Día De Muertos

The living make merry
in fiestas abundant -
the dead crave
a celebration too -
a day of revelry
dedicated to the departed
in Latin culture
the day of the dead -
Día de Muertos.

San Miguel de Allende
in the heart of Mexico
and the heart
of the ancient city,
its twin spired church,
cobble-stoned square
brimming with
makeshift altars
offerings of food
flowers plenty
incense sticks
garlands around portraits
of the departed.

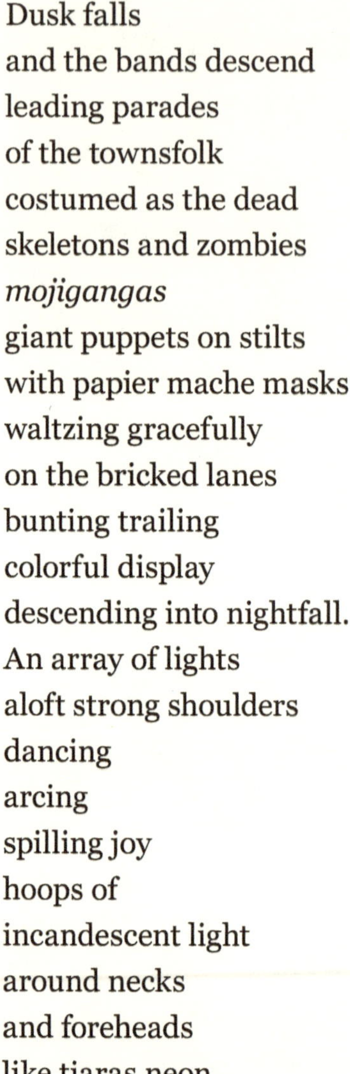

Dusk falls
and the bands descend
leading parades
of the townsfolk
costumed as the dead
skeletons and zombies
mojigangas
giant puppets on stilts
with papier mache masks
waltzing gracefully
on the bricked lanes
bunting trailing
colorful display
descending into nightfall.
An array of lights
aloft strong shoulders
dancing
arcing
spilling joy
hoops of
incandescent light
around necks
and foreheads
like tiaras neon.

The vendors delight
counting pesos
homeward bound
a day of profit
in the name of the dead.

Roadside cafes full
midnight suppers
coffee strong
aromatic, inviting
churros in flavors
and toppings
your taste desires.

Services in the cathedral
ongoing communion
to bless
a rich recitation
of scriptures
a congregation spell-bound
faith deeply rooted
a people steeped
in culture ancient
honoring
the living
and the dead.

B 33
Pandemic

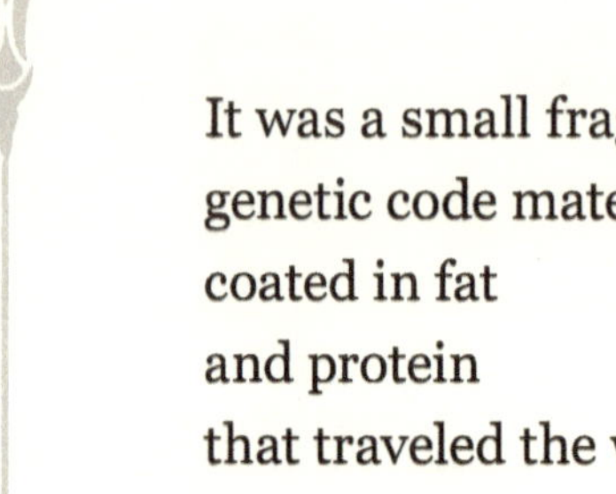

It was a small fragment -
genetic code material
coated in fat
and protein
that traveled the world,
stowaway on
hosts unsuspecting
felling multitudes,
riding others as vehicles
to cast a pall of doom
over a world susceptible.

A plague unknown
origin defined
pointed fingers of blame
physicians and nurses
supporting health workers
the new army
in the trenches
hospitals the battle ground
the Somme offensive again
Crimean massacre
taking bullets
of spittle and sneezes

unmasked zealots
spreading the vapor
malignant.

Scientists and statisticians
burrowed in labs and libraries
searching for answers and cures.
Physicians experimenting
educated trials of commission
better an effort to treat
before death
than watch the helpless
waning of the last breath.

Crooked entrepreneurs
sensing opportunity
hoarding
a run on basic essentials
queues to enter stores
panic buying of loo paper,
sewing masks
a new cottage industry
hawkers no longer
with flower bouquets
at street corners
brandishing instead
designer masks colorful.

Elected officials
active in some states
mayors and governors

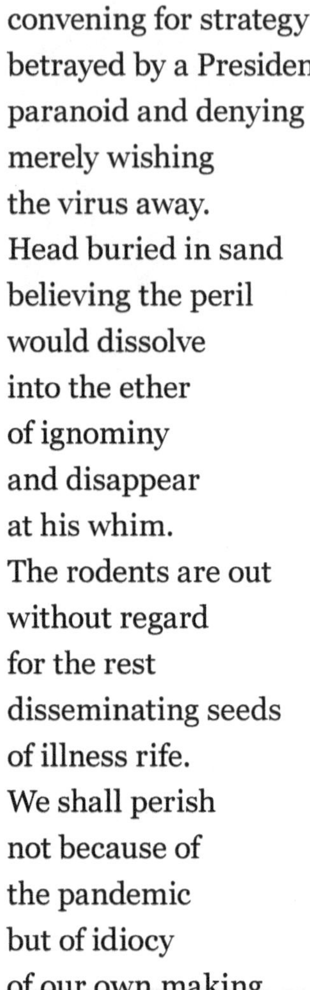
convening for strategy
betrayed by a President
paranoid and denying
merely wishing
the virus away.
Head buried in sand
believing the peril
would dissolve
into the ether
of ignominy
and disappear
at his whim.
The rodents are out
without regard
for the rest
disseminating seeds
of illness rife.
We shall perish
not because of
the pandemic
but of idiocy
of our own making.

B 34

Gray Walls Of Stone Dressed

Gray walls of stone dressed,
gathering dust over decades
silently bearing witness
as events unfold
over miles of foot-steps
and millions of magical moments.

Eager tykes, in blue blazers new,
stifled, collars constrained, neck-ties
strange, milling around
bulletin boards virgin,
bearing notification
of class-rooms assigned
and subjects defined.

The smell of fresh desks,
new text-books distributed,
weighing shoulders slender.
Discipline new,
surroundings new,
concepts and teachers new,
witnessed in silence
by gray walls of stone dressed.

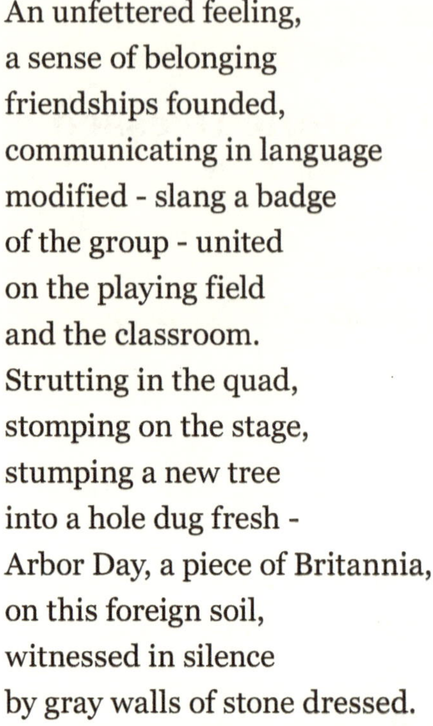

An unfettered feeling,
a sense of belonging
friendships founded,
communicating in language
modified - slang a badge
of the group - united
on the playing field
and the classroom.
Strutting in the quad,
stomping on the stage,
stumping a new tree
into a hole dug fresh -
Arbor Day, a piece of Britannia,
on this foreign soil,
witnessed in silence
by gray walls of stone dressed.

Sad reality - the departure -
of annual batch after batch,
for shores abroad,
witnessed in stifled silence,
by gray walls of stone dressed.

B 35

Mahamrityunjaya

Sitting cross-legged
on a lion skin rug
eyes flickering
in meditation
facing a shrine
in his room -
idols of his
benefactor deities
adorned in
silky finery
rose attar scented
specked with
daubs of vermillion -
he mumbles mantras
in a faint whisper,
supplicant
for the benefit
of those
suctioned into
the vortex
of destiny forlorn.

His eyes open
forehead furrowed
blankness on his face

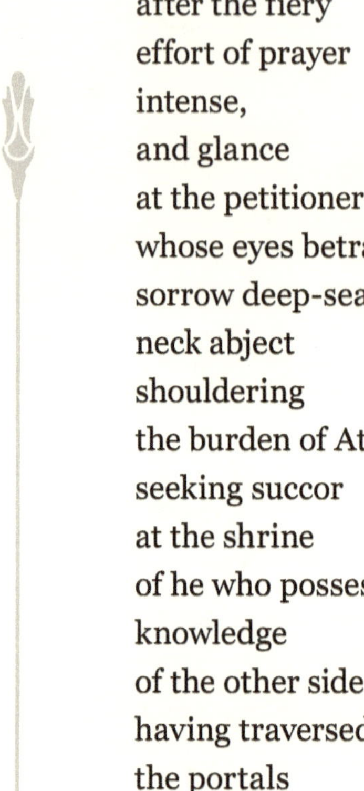

regaining composure
cooling off
after the fiery
effort of prayer
intense,
and glance
at the petitioner
whose eyes betray
sorrow deep-seated,
neck abject
shouldering
the burden of Atlas
seeking succor
at the shrine
of he who possesses
knowledge
of the other side
having traversed
the portals
to Rudra's domain
spanning dimensions
infinite.
He speaks
not like a saint
nor a sage
but a habitué
attuned to matters
mundane
advising the donning
of garb of a certain tinge
and wearing gemstones

to quarry energies
dormant and unused.

Rubies - not blood red
of synthetic origin
but the opaque
crimson hued
mined in Burma
to placate
the Sun God
and bathe in His
life assertive forces.

Cat's eye and citronia,
dual response
for Rahu and Ketu
triangularly crafted
corals
all to negate
effects malicious.

Yellow sapphires
and blue sapphires
assuage Jupiter
and Saturn
according to charts
of complex
planetary apogee.

Diamonds touching
the skin
to awaken

the spark of
impulse
and pearls
to calm
a wandering
mind.

He advocates
rituals
to replenish life
with joy, and health
of body and mind,
to seek a boon
at Shiva's feet
of a life, long -
ward off demise
premature,
redemption
through chanting
the mantra
Mahamrityunjaya -
Shiva's articulation
Shivani -
passed by sages ancient
for the salvation
of humanity.

B 36

Who Wants To Live Forever

Zanzibar born
buck toothed
attitude brash
gamboling and strutting
his wiry frame
inviting
seducing
his audience
into screams frenzied,
throwing
his voice
amplified
modulated
low notes whispered
a pitch sky-high
asking God
in an Innuendo
to answer why?

Rhapsody Bohemian
painting a canvas
wide with imagery
sound boundless
galloping and flitting
teasing with feathers light

thumping incessantly
talent unleashed
unconventional accompaniment
geniuses at their craft.

Serenading the microphone
waltzing with the boom
stomping the boards
Wembley makes
everyone a champion
and the world awaits
its turn
to be enthralled.
Universal appeal
adulation complete ;
these indeed
The Days of Our Lives.

The clouds darken
the grim reaper
earth bound
stricken with
the dreaded plague
when hope is gone
seeking Mother Love -
Mama Please Let Me Back Inside.

Felled
strings fading
drum roll warbling
into oblivion

Empty Spaces
What are We Living For?
The show
the Show Must Go On.

Chapter C

VISHNU

C1
Anant Vishnu

Vishnu's *Yog Nidra*
celestial sleep
quiescence
in tranquility sublime
on the endless coils
of *Shesha Naaga*
the serpent of time
afloat
the milky universe
the *Ksheer Saagar.*

Vishnu opens his eyes
the onset of creation
life through Brahma
himself aloft
a lotus whorl
of a thousand petals
arising from
the seed of
Vishnu's navel.

In Vishnu envisages Brahma
the Being Cosmic - *Vishwarupa*
encompassing the universe whole.
Vishnu, with the one cosmic soul
the one with the two genders and

the three strides of time -
dawn, noon, and dusk.
Endowed with the Vedas
four volumes of divine knowledge;
the five elements - fire his discus
water his lotus, wind his conch
earth his mace and his entirety
ether, permeating space.
Vishnu, the cosmic substance
Prakriti,
matter giving shape to existence,
Vishnu, the cosmic essence
Purusha,
attributing meaning to life
through philosophy and *darshanas*
for self-realization.
Vishnu, master of vitality,
of emotions and directions,
vocations and planes of existence.
Vishnu, Lord of the zodiac and
the lunar asterisms - *nakshatras.*
Vishnu, the master of 108 spirits.
Vishnu - *Vastu Purusha* - Lord of space,
Yuga Purusha - Lord of time.
Infinite, with every action
countered with reaction
congruence at the point of origin
and the point of termination.
Vishnu termed *Bhagwan* -
the totality of the cosmos.

Vishnu - having ten *avatars*
born to restore balance
evolution, from fish to turtle,
to boar and man-lion.
From the dwarf Vamana
to the fierce Parshurama,
from the dutiful prince Rama
to the righteous cowherd Krishna.
From the sage Buddha to
the redeemer Kalki.

Vishnu in tandem with Shiva
Hari-Har coordinating the cycle
of destruction – *pralaya* - the period
of *Yog Nidra* and Shiva's *Tandava,*
dance of destruction,
before Vishnu opens his eyes
and the cycle
begins again.

C 2

Sahasra Dhara

The scorching swelters
of Delhi left behind.
The swamp cooling
efforts of moist
Kush grass screens
left behind.
The hills offer
a sanctuary
from the brutal
heat of the plains.

I, a traveler trekking
the Himalayan foothills
your company,
transient as it is,
enriching the experience
as I learn about
the Gharwali culture
understand the land
of my ancestors.
Through forests
of Birch and Juniper
Blue Fir and Rhododendron
on to Dehra Dun
bridgehead for Musoorie
and Sahasra Dhara
a thousand springs

endowing the Baldi River
sulphur water
dripping from stalactites
water falls gentle
pools by nature
fashioned
to soak in and absorb
the healing qualities
of minerals Himalayan.

Cool waters
quench the thirst
of a body seared
refreshed
to join pilgrims
at Shiva's temple
introspective
balm for a
knotted mind.

Uncoiled energy
drawn towards
the ancient cave
where Dronacharya
for boons meditated
mastery of skills
for peace and war.
Sahasra Dhara
opening a thousand
pores in
my aching body
and uncurling
a thousand thoughts
in my muddled mind.

C 3

Sounds Of Silence Revisited

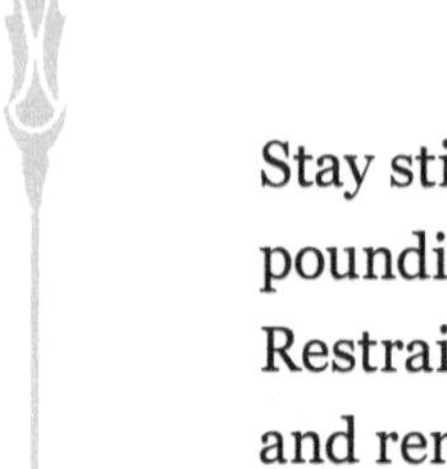

Stay still
pounding heart.
Restrain
and reminisce
recollect walking
up the hill
along the narrow path
amid gorse and bramble
thistle abloom
in a sea of
dotted violet.
Romance in the air
her sweet smell
beside you.

Stay still
pounding heart.
Refrain
thoughts of loneliness
now in the autumn
of life
traversing seasons
approaching
the winter solstice -
white

ashen face
shroud white
of ice and snow
earth imprisoned
cold and muzzled
echoing
sounds of silence
incessant.

Stay still
pounding heart.
Contain
within the expanse
of memory intact
the spring
of daffodils and dahlias
the scent
of her auburn hair
walks verdurous
lush leafy love
flourishing afresh.
Whispered
sounds of silence.

Stay still
pounding heart.
Sustain
flowing along meridians
matrices of energy
forces of life
mobile ever forward

beyond the hilltops
peaks introducing
other higher pinnacles
still to reach
and then
spatial span.
Sounds of silence
supreme.

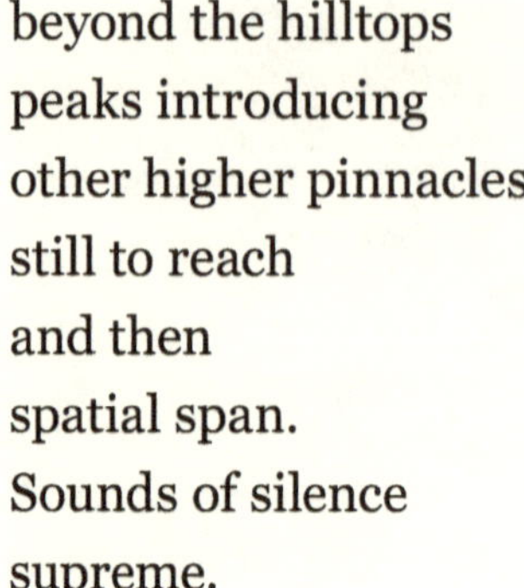

C 4

The Nun

Petite
walking along
the corridors
of the hospital
attitude angelic
healing halo
her habit
a Catholic commitment
comforting and calming
discordant health,
assuaging the ravages
of pain.
Yet the novice
balks at the prospect
of a life cloistered
part of an order
steeped in denial
of the self.
Doubts abound -
service is not
in arbitration;
vows of responsibility
weighed on the scales
of a present constricted
but the promise of

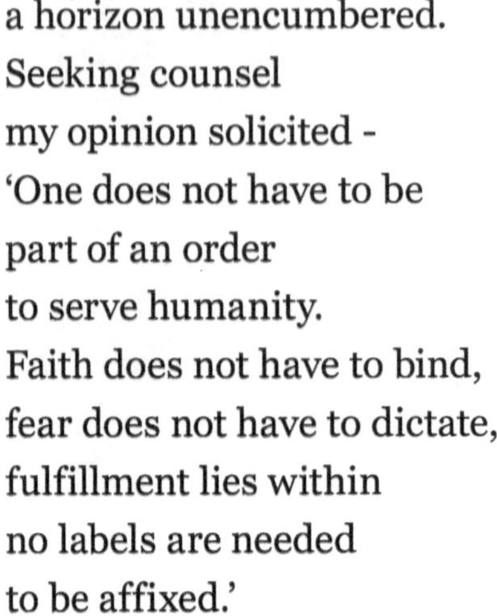

a horizon unencumbered.
Seeking counsel
my opinion solicited -
'One does not have to be
part of an order
to serve humanity.
Faith does not have to bind,
fear does not have to dictate,
fulfillment lies within
no labels are needed
to be affixed.'

She opts out of vows final
discards the habit dark
letting her hair down
walks on the beach
for once enjoying
the summer breeze
decently unclad
free of bonds
but willingly
donning responsibility
walking towards a future
self-assigned.

C 5
Muse # 9

You do not
answer summons
to the common phone
tucked near the entrance
of your residential block.
I know you are back
from your day
at the training hospital
and must have received
messages posted for you.

Waiting for your call
hanging near my phone
unsettling -
distraction,
a walk in the drizzly evening
clad in coat warm
umbrella in hand
dusk reflected
in wet cobblestones
of the street.

The light
in your room
at the students' hostel
is switched on -

your window a faint glow
in the dank air
as I stand below
watching and waiting
to catch a glimpse
of you
when you will
draw the drapes
of your window.

C 6

The Thespian

Gray images blurred
aged negatives scratched
projection 16 mm
on a blunted screen.
Dev Das shuffling
across the set
chewing the scenery -
tragic hero
whispering his lines
erudite and translucent
fans gasping in wonder
as he penetrates
the depth of their psyche.

A son of the soil
swashbuckling rake
supplicant in the temple
lovelorn prince
accidental leader
and union chief
prancing along a train
on a narrow hilly track,
the thespian weaves magic
craft enchanting mellifluously
underplaying emotion

eye-brow raised quizzically
cowering with fear
towering majestically
conflicted with self
conforming with society
exiting the silver screen
adorning billboards
burnishing pages printed.

He sits across me
inspiring adulation
as I feign confidence
and spar with words
gently nudging
towards answers mundane
but his mastery excels
overpowering exposition
as philosophy and geography
history and humor
radiate to enrich
an interview assigned
for ten minutes -
extended ten-fold
blessed his words;
or my ears
that heard them?

C 7

Wandering Players

A chance meeting
a struggling actor
a promising writer
visionaries both
pioneers
sowing fields furrowed
in a community
culturally crimped -
taking on the challenge
to convert and inspire
artistic expression abundant.
Coffee house theaters
inuring the side streets
off Normandie and Vermont
Hollywood witnessing
the birth
of fringe theater -
playwrights alien
idiom alien
account alien
but emotion universal.

Tagore, Sir no More -
as Britain oppressed India -
his reversal of knighthood

dramatized.
Silence, the Court is in Session -
happenings in Bombay -
staged half a world
away;
and adaptations
Barefoot in the Park -
A View from the Bridge -
the stage an outlet
for souls struggling.

A band of actors
of disparate origin
passion identical
movement fluid
speech silver
silence pregnant
attention rapt.
We move on,
the boards
have been trodden
lights extinguished
playbills neglected
memorabilia dusty -
it's bound to happen;
actors don't die
just run out
of lines.

C 8

Sounds Of Africa

Tradition
rooted deep
in the soil
in the village
in the tribe
ululating sounds
blowing of horns crude
percussion of drums
of a different pitch and timbre
tom toms
derisively simplistic
a colonial term
failing to understand
rhythm infective
inducting dance
unrefined, but of the soil
at one with nature.

Tradition
songs
to celebrate
rites of passage
songs
to galvanize warriors
spur to leave as boys

and return as men.

Sounds of Africa
discovered and globalized
voices enthralling
the silken Belafonte
the alluring Makeba
the Black Blood's seductive
Aie a Mwana.

The world
discovers Africa
yet fails to see
the wood for the trees
attempting to codify
a continent vast
minimized to
a reference miniscule.
The sound African
instrumentation universal
soul African
Osibisa taking London
by storm
Ipi Tombi the world
making Africa
a marketing commodity
but tradition
rooted deep
in the soil
and the village
and the tribe.

C 9
Cruising Kenya

Saturday morning drive
to the farmlands of Limuru
to get fresh produce
from the red soil fertile.
Flavorful tomatoes
crispy string beans
peas sweet and succulent
spinach and lettuce

to adorn the shelves
at an uncle's
green grocery - *Kikapu.*
My favorite,
gigantic green guavas
sweet and fleshy
with seeds soft
and taste hallowed.

Sunday morning drive
an arboretum in Kiambu
not as grand
as the Nairobi one
but attractive
in its vicinity -
a coffee estate
aromatic berries ready

plucked and processed
hilly country
gently beguiling
blue skies invigorating.

Weekly drive
school Land-rover
through the Rift Valley
past the quaint church
on the escarpment
built by Italian
prisoners of war;
stopping for a snack -
Rawal's in Nakuru -
through fields of pyrethrum
Aberdare Hills, Mau Summit
Londiani, off a fork
on the main road;
through the township, Kedowa
on to the Tea Hotel
Kericho, the brew's capital
undulating hills
lush with tea shrubs
neat rows stretching
far to the horizon
as clouds punctually
gather for
the afternoon downpour.
Ahero Plain
seen from the summit
Lake Victoria shimmering

like a mirror
hot near the equator
Kisumu on the lake.
A visit with aging relatives
and drive to the Hippo Point
before driving
onto Busia
on the Uganda border.
Leprosy being studied
a W.H.O. project
gratifying, as is
the dusty clinic
at Mumias, memorable
for its lone mango tree
laden with green fruit
tart and tongue tingling
seasoned with chili and salt.
Cruising Kenya
destinations varied
taking one
in its fold
enwombs protectively
preserving memories
for recollection future.

C 10

Fort Jesus

Overnight journey
by sleeper train
from Nairobi - exciting
an adventure when
the company comprises
a coterie of convivial
cousins.
Early morning arrival
hot and humid coast
Mombasa island inviting.

No visit to the coast
complete without
a stop at the only fort
in the country.
Gray walls ascending
lichen covered in places
sentinel to the entrance
of the old harbor -
a placid ocean
dhows plying trade
keeping Mombasa afloat.
The might of the Portuguese
established - guarding
trade routes to the East

keeping the Swahili coast
under control firm.
Tussles and counter attacks
Omani challenges from a Sultan
finding anchor in Zanzibar.
Conquerors displaced
new colonizers in place
the fort becomes
a prison, but cannot
contain the movement
self-rule and independence.
Powers crumble as do
symbols of their might -
museums and monuments
to gawk at, comment on.
Piles of shot rusting
canons pointing seawards
rooms lined with cases
artifacts preserved
roped off balustrades
in the rear, brittle
under restoration;
avoiding fatality
as a careless cousin
leaning over, pulled back
in the nick of time.
Enjoying packed lunches
admiring the view
across the harbor
awaiting the evening
as the grounds outside

become foot-ball fields,
and amblers enjoy
the cool breeze
walking under the shadow
of the mighty walls
of Fort Jesus.

C 11

Rain Drops Dancing

Los Angeles
usually parched
hillsides lush
no more
skies opaque
under a shroud
of a smog sorrel
but when
the skies open
faucets of nature
the waters plunge
El Nino empowered
to revitalize
a city seared.

Monday morning
usual disincentive
commuting to
a job imperative.
Pummeling rain
almost keeps me home
but responsibility supreme.
Raincoat-clad
hoodie in place
glasses dotted

droplets forming lenses
creating images
symphonic
reflected lights
dancing
as I place
my briefcase
in the trunk.
I glance
at the window opposite
and am gratified
to see your smiling face
bidding adieu
silently,
the glimpse
to recollect
as I labor through
the routine
of the working day.

C 12
Epic Lean

Epics were born
in Hollywood
but the greatest purveyor
of tales grand
emanated from
the British sensitivity
of Lean - David Lean.

Vast cinemascope landscape
elephants ponderous
against the skyline
a dusty introduction
Passage to India
caves dark
an enigma
like the country
dominated by the Raj
protecting its own
sacrificing the native
for matters pristine
of pigment.

The initial structure rickety
retro-fitted and trussed
abandoned
a new construction

to withstand
military might massive
on the railway
Bridge on the River Kwai.
Treachery and plans
to escape
yet constructing
their own doom
to the strains
of Colonel Bogey's March.

A young Lara
Zhivago's love
subjected to exploitation
for the sins of a mother -
stains of blood
on a fresh bed of snow
symbolic of her despoilment.
Revolution
brother against brother
separated families searching
finding only disappointment.
A curved Urals road
a troika traveling towards
respite temporary
lovers united
divided
human saga garnished
with sprigs of reality.

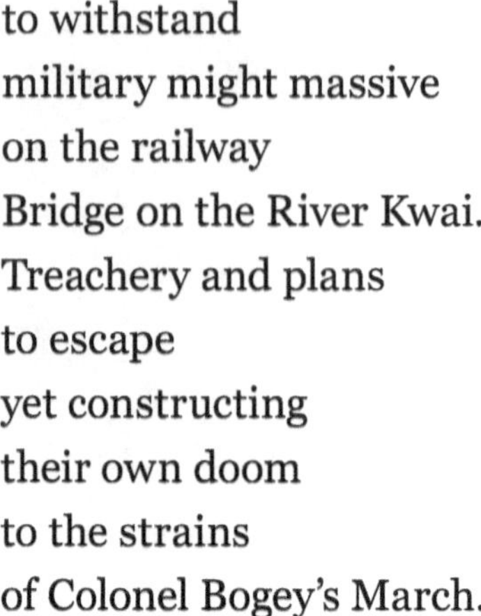

The bluffs
and the cliffs
pebbly beaches
wind eerily cruising
along the Irish coast
County Cork captured
critically caressed
Ryan's Daughter
protective parasol
against bright light
deflected off
the golden sand
nimbly stepping
into a life
of patriotism
and intrigue.

On a country road
a lonely motor-bike
character intense
a long mane
on a sculpted face
wind-blown
rides into oblivion.
Fade in
sand dunes
two lonely camels
miniscule
growing in stature
man, at war,
with himself,

and man
at war -
Lawrence of Arabia
blowing up trains
leading hordes
horsemen kicking sand
on a spree of destruction
self-exploration
gone awry.

Epics
craftily painted
using the medium
of light and shadows
captured through
lenses prime
on film to be projected
to an audience
exalted.

C 13

Belle Vue

Belle Vue
a new word
in the lexicon
of Nairobi denizens -
not just
a drive-in cinema
but an icon
social and cultural.

Tuesday night specials
entrance ticketed
only for the cars
crammed and cramped
necks craning
to glimpse
the screen gigantic -
an angled wall
at the edge of
a speakers-fitted
parking lot.
Concessions
an excuse for
a chilled Tusker or Pilsner
covered rows
of stadium seating

seldom used
but absorbing
the overflow
of crowded cars.

Sundays
a time for social exchange
vehicles parked
in designated bays
speakers tested
ere the start
of the latest fare
from a bountiful Bollywood.
An escape
en-masse from the cars
as the out-door cinema
becomes a circuit
for ambling walkers
stopping, greeting, gossiping
surreptitious exchanged glances
giggling girls and guys
frolicking in clusters
flamboyant
pea-cocks displaying
finery seductive.
Such a culture
uniquely endemic
to the city and people
seeking expression
in an age of innocence
sans a deceptive veneer

an age of openness
sans an attitude pompous
an age of camaraderie
in a community
inclusive.

Dusk and darkness
return to waiting cars
setting up of recorders
to tape musical tracks
as the romances
and the thrillers
flicker on the screen.

The show's over.
A collective noise
of engines starting
revving to egress
strategies to negotiate
bottlenecks to tackle
and join the main highway
for the drive home.

C 14

Muse # 10

Adolescent dreams
fantasies stellar
though surges hormonal
disable discretion,
a modicum
of decency prevails;
shyness innate
tongue-tied
never able to express
feelings for you.

You were in the same
class at school
yet we were never
assigned the same projects;
you remained an enigma.
You lived in the locality
two houses away
and though I saw you
walking to the shops
never had the courage
to stop and say hello.

You graduated
to another school,
another country,

to settle and study
following your father's
retirement.
You remained a memory
mysterious - a childhood
crush tucked away
in a remote corner
of my mind
till a chance visit
with a common friend
to a house in Manchester -
it happened to be
your parents'
and for the first time
meeting you after ages
I was able to approach
and say hello.

C 15
Stratford Upon Avon

My children
love the country
having discovered
its charms urbane -
London inviting exploration
and the rural counties
on further probing
a garnish
on the rich tradition
of culture,
of Shakespeare,
whose works
have been seen
at the Globe.

A leisurely drive
on the Cotswold
country lanes to
Stratford-upon-Avon -
a humble cottage
Anne Hathaway linked
rooms where literature
was created.
A town serene
dipped in the nectar
of esthetics sweet -

walks along the streets
stopping for tea and scones
English fudge and
nougats delectable,
commenting on girls
with low slung jeans
and peeping
seductive thongs.
Rowing on the Avon
steering the boat
under arched bridges
'Watch out
your oar hit
the poor swan!'
my girls exclaim,
as their mother chides
for carelessness;
grinning and making light
of the event as
great oarsman-ship
is sheepishly truncated.
Morris dancers
indigenous talent
born of the soil
entertaining
in the town square.
Indian lunch at Balti,
refueled for
a sunny afternoon
soaking in
the Bard's town.

C 16
Llangollen

The edge
of the Berwyn Range
valley hollowed out of
limestone escarpment
welcoming Welsh
hamlet of Llangollen.

A ruined abbey
peeping at a park
caravans arranged
in a horse-shoe fashion
playground
the enclosed lea;
our little girl
learning to ride
a bike
falling, grazing knees
persistent
chased
by adopted uncle
and gran-ma
benefactors from
an age past.

Uphill walks
chasing lambs

as amused
farmhands watch,
reaching a fish farm
cultured trout
imported tilapia.
Narrow paths
avoiding nettles
reaching the center
of town
enjoying savory chips
seated on a bench
on the banks
of River Dee.

Country roads
tooting local trains
eskers on limestone hills
Snowdon the crowning glory.
Welsh north coast
Conwy Castle
canons on balustrades
steep steps into
towers dank.
Gray sea uninviting
as a long day
of summer
casts shadows long
dampness creeps in
as caravan awaits
sleep after
a day sapping.

C 17
Lakeland Allure

Walls of misshapen rocks
balanced upon each other
separating lush fields
dotted with grazing sheep
occasional cottage
chimney belching wisps
of gentle smoke
sailing smoothly towards
fells and tarns
pulchritude picturesque
Cumbria blessed
lakes with water
resplendent.

Ferry over Windermere
forming clouds
over the evening skies
warmth of a hearth
waiting
hot mugs of cocoa
gazing at the waters
swallow the horizon
into ebony darkness.

Driving on the narrow roads
Ullswater bound

gorse covered hills
splashes of flowers wild
enticing paths
inviting a stop
discovery of scents
a pastoral communion
with nature.

Ambling over hills
climbing over stiles
gamboling with the sheep
breathing the life force
of air pure and fresh
stop at the local pub
ploughman's lunch
soaking in tales of
local folklore.

Cockermouth manse,
with a view to envy
sprawling estate
Erato for Wordsworth-
florid fields feeding
imagination
paradise descended
on earth
and fashioned
this haven
of Lakeland allure.

C 18

Crawling Pubs

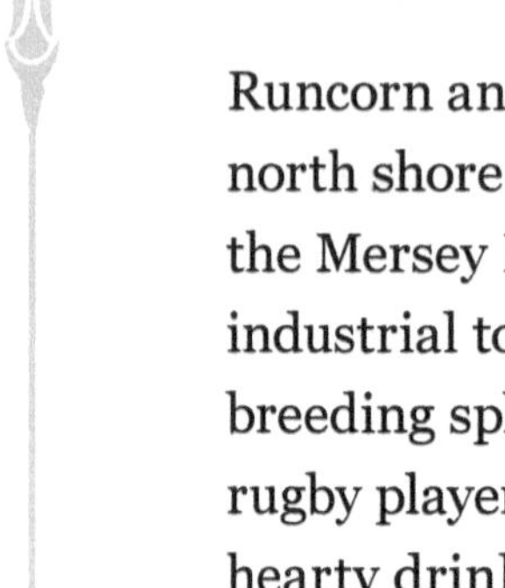

Runcorn and Widnes
north shore of
the Mersey River
industrial towns
breeding splendid
rugby players,
hearty drinkers
keeping the pubs
in fiscal health.
Gathering spots
for social discourse
the neighborhood's
living room
gossip and news
exchanged
before the patrons
return to cold
and congested homes
and the drear
of drudgery.

For friends visiting
the North
escape from London's
loud belching traffic,

tempting attraction
crawling through
quaint watering holes
along the Mersey Canal -
places for a pint
and animated conversation
planning adventures next,
discovering North Wales
the Wirral, Cheshire,
Southport affluent
and a sojourn
to the lights
of Blackpool.

Pubs near the ferry
of Warrington town
barges on the river
locks on the canal
tow paths intact
Manchester connected
healthy country lunches
a pint of bitter
smoke-filled rooms
dart boards pierced
lively noise
friendly banter
time to be driven
to another label
another Publican's
premises eccentric.

C 19

Lllandings

(In recognition of **"Triple L"** by **Devika Syal**)

LONDON

Flight, twin propeller plane, protracted
over arid Africa and urbane Europe -
Heathrow landing
as the red orb turns orange,
dawn as the city grumbles,
grudging the end of night
as the gatekeepers of the nation
pencil in another cross -
fresh immigrant, fatigued but fascinated,
driven - barren roads, red asphalt, borders lush,
monuments awakening memories
Empire dissolved, statuesque sentinels
guarding the monarchy within, palace imposing,
Big Ben striking, towering
the chambers of governance,
as the Bull-Dog PM
stoops, silently brooding,
reflections in the late summer Thames,
and the bridge over
to an unadorned city, stirring
for Saturday merchandizing.
Side-walk stalls, fruit on barrows,

cloth by the yard, spilling
from boots of cars,
and dialect, unfamiliar
a loud, sonorous litany
as custom is sought.

Culture shock
tank-tops and hot pants
merrily trotting -
the sun draws them out
as red double-deckers
deposit mothers and children
on crowded pavements.
The city languorous no more
fertile vibrations in sync
with my seeking mind
as I become
part of the Main.

LOS ANGELES

Canadian city by the lake
tamed by a snowstorm
sinking into a bed white
powder packed
flurries coating afresh
thorny icicles descending
from pregnant eaves.
A memorable day
to leave all behind;
plane de-iced -

the Pacific awaits,
noon time sun, mirage like,
reflecting shimmering rays
off the plane's wing,
as the ocean heaves
and wheels touch tarmac.
Nothing lax about LAX.
Movement serpentine
vehicles threading the 405
winter jacket shed
warmth percolates.
Wilshire off ramp
Santa Monica
a slice of Britannia,
straddling pub culture,
brief respite
Pasadena beckons,
as the city fades behind -
a glide over
Eisenhower's gift,
the first highway laid,
an artery to homes
majestic, dwarfed amid
palms tall and avenues broad,
manicured lawns
hedges of rose,
air crisp -
an island of altruism,
within the pulsating chaos
of the metropolis maternal,
anachronism,

post war serenity,
and vibrations attuned
to the voice of a soul
finding home.

LAS VEGAS

The mood euphoric
suspended expectation,
the road inviting
new experience.
The desert surrounding,
assailed by deluge -
flash-flood testing
nerves and patience -
a passing fury
sunlight again
blazing bright
and looming
over the horizon,
glimmering,
levitating,
towers of concrete
indistinctly distinct,
refuge for the weary
and those wearily
seeking weariness
wading through casinos
all night long.
The glitz hits
garish at close quarters

gigantic cut-outs,
cacti and slippers,
cow-boy hats on girls,
stardust a-twinkle,
Aladdin and Dunes,
Sahara and Flamingo
a palace purportedly
Caesar's,
a huge clown beckoning
a circus of sorts.
All drowned
in a cacophony
of coins hitting
collecting trays of tin,
bandits' arms arcing achingly
a new patina released.
This soul sought solitude
but solitude is serenaded
by noise - alluring noise
mesmerizing noise,
enticing noise,
harmonized waves,
stepping into
the fantasy of
self-making.
What happens
in this oasis
stays in this oasis

REFRAIN

Recounting,
relating,
repeating,
little fingers
holding onto
mine,
walking familiar
avenues
spanning space
and time,
reliving
through
eyes and ears new
vibrations new,
these cities,
my lady loves,
transduce into
words uttered
by daughters
in harmony
with feelings felt
decades before.

C 20

Celebrating A Brother Departed

All that remain
after fifty years
of removal
are your memories
and your portrait
that guides me
through life
smiling down on me
as I sit at my desk.

Childhood
shared admiring
your collection
of postage stamps
and post cards
carefully secreted
in a safe place.

Narrating stories
dramatically enhanced
swashbuckling princes
fairy tales
morality parables
Panchatantra

animated
religious heroes
coming alive
through the pages
of the Urdu *Martand*
you read from.

A partner and companion
for movies of adventure
Steve Reeves as Hercules
Rob Taylor as Ivanhoe
Dara Singh
in wrestling titles
Saturday morning
matinees -
young boys' stuff.

Your penchant
for music
carefully compiling lists
songs of a certain motif
for Chaman's
or Soni's shows
on Kenya radio
winning competitions;
current on the latest hits
courtesy Radio Ceylon's
Binaca Geetmala
with Amin Sayani.

Friend loyal

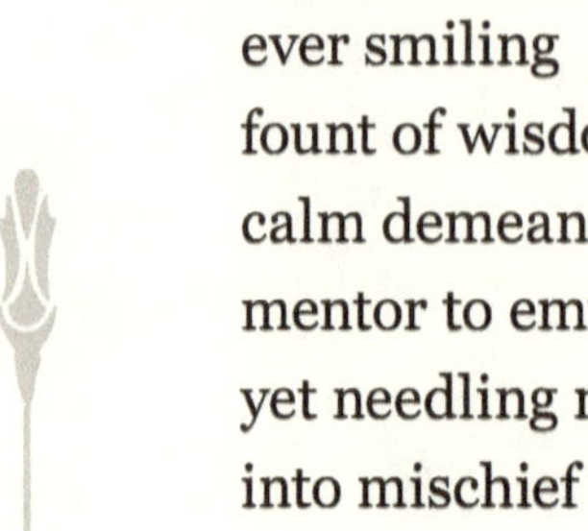

counseling peers
sagacity innate
ever smiling
fount of wisdom
calm demeanor
mentor to emulate
yet needling me
into mischief
and arguments mundane.

Travel companion
riding rough shod
crowded Indian trains
cautiously practical
discovering places
fresh
Shalimar Gardens
in Sri Nagar
the meadows
at Pahalgam
riding horses
from Gulmarg
to reach glaciers Himalayan
at Khilanmarg
admiring Kashmiri beauty
at Kheer Bhavani
circumambulating
Lake Wullar.
Shikara rides on the Dal
picnic at Char Chinar
climbing Shankaracharya Hill

exploration and discovery
of self and terrain.

Always in demand
at Indian weddings
at community venues
as we volunteered
to supervise arrangements
service and skills
organizational
assets inherent.

Your ambition
was perhaps stinted
victim of convention
staying home
to tend the family.
You expressed dreams
for me to accomplish
ascend heights
you could not
prodding always
in encouragement
taking pride
in any triumph.

Zorba the Greek
the last film
we saw together
etched in memory
never to forget

the last evening
of our time together.

The tears that were shed
shed no more
the void you left
void no more
your example
has inspired growth
I've lived each day
celebrating your life
reading letters
you left behind
recollecting memories
an element
of my private self.
Words written
songs composed
roles enacted
applying
the healing touch
all a celebration
of your being.

C 21
Maui

Snug
in the Hawaiian
archipelago
Maui
two islands
conjoined at the waist
topographically different
offering experiences
varied.
Pineapple and
passion fruit parfaits
juice of sugarcane
squeezed fresh
mangoes juicy
sweet as honey,
under the majestic shadow
of inert Haleakala.

Early morning drive
winding roads ascending
the volcano extinct
a clan of bikers
keeping apace
steadily up the hill.
The wind

cold and clear
on the summit
cracking dawn
a burst
of saffron sun
semi-lighting
the crater's bowl
crescentic cusp
revealing scape lunar.
Wind sculptured
wilderness smooth
sinking systematically
paths crisscrossing
for those who dare
to descend into
the valley desolate.

The morning clear
the ocean cerulean
a wisp beyond
lush vegetation
on the rain-ward side.
My companion in tow
dreading the curvy
road to Hana
broken
washed away
by deluges tropical
craters to avoid
narrow bridges
over pregnant streams

waterfalls cascading
gossamer threads
in the sunlight
through vegetation dense
pools formed
icy clear water
flora affluent
mango trees
and guavas pink
tropical paradise flirting
with the ocean placid.
And Hana
miles of silver sand
inviting relaxation
forgetting the ordeal
of arrival.

C 22

The Pathologists

The auditorium
full of eager students
striving to become doctors
a barrage of information
cadavers paving the way
to exploration without formalin.
First meeting
a rookie lecturer
fresh from training abroad.
Petite pretty pathologist
contrary to expectation
of a buff butcher
of a man.
A lilting voice
accent struggling
between native tongue
and acquired inflections
from across the seas.
A drab subject
made interesting
beauty an incentive
to attend her sessions.

Years later
following a multitude
of countries and hospitals
pathologists again

delegated to train
the science of detecting
that which is abnormal
placing structure
to organic damage
understanding the genesis
of disease.

The chief of the group
ex Air Force Captain
earned position relaxing
teaching and management -
a myriad of matters
non-medical.
Chain-smoking
anathema for the one
dissecting sooty lungs
relating stories
of theaters of war
and of his penchant
for writing tawdry romances
under a nom de plume.

His assistant
my mentor
another smoker
always in scrub-suits
wearing a Chicago attitude
on his sleeve
devouring coffee
by the urnful
peering down
a microscope

deciphering dysfunction
dictation sounding
poetic.

Thrown into the deep end
the basement
of the hospital
the morgue and
the autopsies suite
debut prosection
with rudimentary instructions
thrown my way.
My first incision scalpeled
with surgical precision
taking non-economic
hours to complete.
Experience sped
the process along
and medical residents
posing questions challenging
handled with poise
and confidence.
The foundation
deep
the concepts
embedded firmly
insight into pathology
visual
abetting a career
in diagnosis
and treatment
making a doctor
better.

C 23

Joined At The Hip

You, my opponent
Hindi elocution competition;
you had the advantage
your uncle a judge, and
your speech penned
by a scholarly neighbor.
Your delivery though
your own
belied
all the help you had mustered
as you persuaded gently
with forceful argument
in language mellifluous
pleasant to hear.
You were
my victorious opponent.

You walked from the pavilion
onto the field
leading student cricketers-
the nation's best
hosting a foreign eleven
batting with focus
slicing and caroming
the ball across the grounds

a sterling victory
a feather in your cap.

You knew not
who I was
but brought together
students in college
sharing the same schedule,
grouped together
by the quirk
of roll numbers
and soon
a relation symbiotic
enriching
each other
and feeding
off each other.

The other's families
became our own
the other's life
constituted our own
I had your back
in your amorous
exploits
and heeded
your advice
in my adventures alike.
You had my back
as I took responsibility
of affairs domestic

and joined as we were
at the hip, you
akin to a brother,
stood beside me
in hour of need.

Life sent us careening
on courses distinct
but security lies
in knowing
you are just
a phone-call away.

C 24

The Phone

Our neighbor
was rich;
he had a phone
installed in his home.
A shiny black unit
with a rotary dial
displaying numbers
bold on ivory background
a tiny lock
fitted through
a dialing slot
preventing
usage unauthorized.
Our neighbor
was rich.
The phone
a symbol of status.

Our neighbor
was cooperative
shared the phone number
with us
and when we
received a call
his son was sent

over to summon.
The line usually
crackled
the hellos usually
shouted
privacy a concept
alien
and the brief call
followed by inquiry
of who called
and what transpired.

Our neighbor
was vigilant
screened all calls
and the ones
inappropriate
cut off and reported
to our parents.

Our neighbor
was posted
to another city
and the facility
to make and
receive calls
came to
an abrupt end.

We needed a phone.
We wanted a phone.

We craved a phone.
We implored.
Father relented
we got a phone.

The unit installed
with lock and all
the pride
of the living room
on a white
lace covered pedestal
all its own.
The parade of calls
started soon
not for us alone
but friendly neighbors too.
The domino effect of
entertaining calls
for brethren -
a community
well-knit
a family extended.

C 25

The Masseuse

Aching muscles
back contorted
out of shape -
picking an empty box
and straightening up
I,n arrested motion
painful ordeal
acute radiculitis
lumbago
sciatica,
whatever the tag
the severity of pain
equally acute.
Massages with Diclofenac
Myoflex, Icy Hot et al
injection of Toradol
all to no effect;
I am averse
to taking opiates
so, suffered
through the night.
Ensuing day
no better
damn Covid 19
the chiropractor
and massage places
all shut.

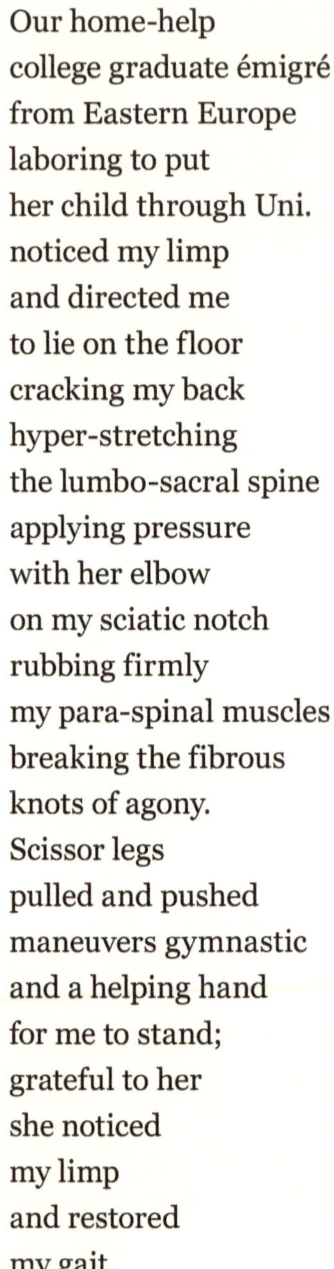

Our home-help
college graduate émigré
from Eastern Europe
laboring to put
her child through Uni.
noticed my limp
and directed me
to lie on the floor
cracking my back
hyper-stretching
the lumbo-sacral spine
applying pressure
with her elbow
on my sciatic notch
rubbing firmly
my para-spinal muscles
breaking the fibrous
knots of agony.
Scissor legs
pulled and pushed
maneuvers gymnastic
and a helping hand
for me to stand;
grateful to her
she noticed
my limp
and restored
my gait.

C 26
Ecstasy

Open grassy grounds vast
some coated
in pulverized *murram*
part of the Railways Gymkhana
and when not in use,
serving as playground
for young kids' games
of their own making;
knocking down
and reconstructing
piles of uneven stones
as a balding tennis ball
thrown, an opponent to tag.
Modified versions
of conventional *kabaddi*
and the occasional
race around the tracks
and the tradition
of football
and field hockey.

Come rainy season
churning of the dirt roads
rivulets carving a passage
through soft and black
loamy soil
slippery to walk on

intentionally slicked
to form a natural slide.
Hurling pointed rods
rebars salvaged
from construction sites
spiking the soft earth
scoring points
teams engaging
friendly rivalries.

Gigantic trenches
dug for building foundations
filled with rain water murky
pools to jump in
roping of planks together
floating makeshift rafts
mud splattered clothes
a wash-day challenge.

Collecting glass marbles
intricate colorful patterns
wagered in games
placed in circular confines
shot at skillfully
attempting to dislodge
just one to win
the booty entire.

Somersaulting on rubber mats
balancing on parallel bars
vaulting over wooden horses
jumping through hoops
fiery wire frames

head-stands without support
walking on one's arms
athletic prowess
a part of growing up.

Eyeing ripe fruit
mangoes and guavas
luscious purple *jamuns*
mulberries hanging in bunches
easy targets to pluck
without express permission
pleasures illicit endearing
chased off occasionally
by an irate gardener;
running away
finding sanctuary
in spaces between homes.

My cousin gets
a new bicycle
brings it to the grounds
flaunting riding feats
'Look Ma, no hands,'
lording over his advantage
letting us ride
after much persuasion
promises of buying him
chips and soda.
Falling, grazing knees
mastery attained
to balance and pedal
towards a state
of childhood ecstasy.

C 27

It Takes A Village

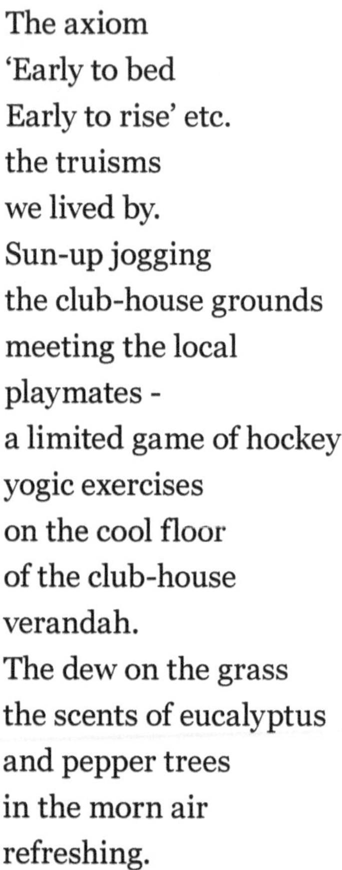

The axiom
'Early to bed
Early to rise' etc.
the truisms
we lived by.
Sun-up jogging
the club-house grounds
meeting the local
playmates -
a limited game of hockey
yogic exercises
on the cool floor
of the club-house
verandah.
The dew on the grass
the scents of eucalyptus
and pepper trees
in the morn air
refreshing.

Breakfast of *parathas*
with mango *achaar*
following the obligatory tablespoon
of mouth-watering paste -
soaked and blanched almonds

leaves of Brahmi Booti -
Bacopa Monnieri -
designed to sharpen wit
and memory sustain.

Neighborhood parents
watching our backs
keeping an eye
on collective safety
an age where
it did take a village
to raise a child
and the child
when older
took care
of the village.

C 28

Childhood Chums

Childhood chums
sharing stories
childhood frolics
climbing mango trees
picking fruit green
salt and chili embellished
tart taste satisfied,
tamarind pods in pockets
sticky and covered in lint,
pepeta fruit fuzzy
once shelled
fingers perennially
stained brown.

Childhood chums
sharing stories
pretense firemen
racing through
the school's quad
narrow corridors
ringing bells
imaginary
putting out fires
imaginary.
Sometimes

train drivers
whistling and tooting
pulling carriages
escarpment
imaginary.

Childhood chums
sharing stories
your family's
migration -
ancestral home
in India.
Tales of Moga
your totemic town,
of the Krishna temple
built by expatriates,
of our brief encounter
as I traveled
through Punjab
on my visit to India.

Childhood chums
sharing stories
days in Dublin
finding romance
and career
finding a new home,
the Canadian outback
creating structures
with your signature
designs.

Childhood chums
sharing stories,
cherishing memories
of an era gone by.

C 29

Adventures In Print

There was an age
when travel was limited
and visual happenings gleaned
from newsreels
before movies;
the world was imagined,
books a window
to far off places.

Childhood fantasies
Scheherzade's tales
Enid Blyton,
racist warts and all,
graduating to
graphic stories
illustrated classics
abridged narrations
heavy tomes condensed
for minds light.

The discovery
of stories original
adolescent anticipation
devouring volumes
as fast as

the McMillan
and Desai libraries
supplied them.

Falling in love
with the image
of Lorna Doone,
walking in the shoes
of Robinson Crusoe,
terrifying nightmares -
Fagin and Uriah Heep,
Tom Brown's privation
at Rugby,
tasting the spray
of an angry sea
Two Years Before the Mast,
capsized adventures
of the Swiss Family Robinson.
Escapades of Alain Quartermain
Africa in a new light
Prester John personified;
romance with Wilkie Collins'
Woman in White
intrigue with Walter Scott.
Eerie mists of Sherlock's cases
troubled tears of Tess
Casterbridge a town tragic,
the History of Mr. Polly,
Captain Nemo
20,000 Leagues Under the Sea
and a League of Gentlemen -

all a part of
weekend reading
sequestered under a quilt
curled on the bottom half
of a cozy bunk bed
and forever affected
by the journey -
adventures in print.

C 30
Muse # 11

Summer evenings extended
inebriated by your presence
Delamere Forest trails inviting
leisurely driving
country lanes
banking and curving
arbors of chestnuts ancient
scented sweet by pines.

Meandering trails
well beaten paths
encroached by blades
of grass fresh
saplings rising
from stray seeds.
Elm and lime
ash, beech, and yew
and oaks majestic
crowning the glory
of the woods ancient.
Birdsong - wrens and jays
matching in melody
our footsteps
and heartbeats
synchronized.

The evening train
to Chester
on the local line
chugging through wilderness
smoke from an engine mature
billowing gently
dispersing
in the mild evening breeze
blowing in from
the Irish Sea.
Resting on the balustrades
watching the train recede
sharing thoughts innermost
absorbed
conversation digested
precursor to the evenings
that lie ahead
as we age together.

C 31

Spirit And Imagination Grand

The wind hot and humid
the Black Mountains foreboding
the Nevada desert arid
the skyline of Loughlin casinos
garish in the distance.
The sound of pennies clanging
the pull of bandits
one armed,
boating on the Colorado
insects humming
joyful whoops
of jet-ski riders,
strolling on the river walk
retiring late in the evening.

The great American tradition
family road-trip of siblings
heading towards Williams
gateway to the Canyon Grand.
The south rim congested
shuttle buses displacing
cars individual.
Driven to the chasm
wonder at nature's carvings
stony sculptures crafted

by waters mighty
of a river receding
and the buffing effect
of noisy gushing winds
as ancient Puebloans
witnessed the transition
of ancestral lands.
Gazing at the rocky buttes
strategic look-out points
mystical names of eastern wisdom
Zoroaster, Vishnu, Shiva
Brahma and Buddha redefined.
The sunlight playing with color
painting the rocky canvas
in different hues
as the orb descends
and shadows engulf
the gorge
inky darkness
eerily silent echoes
of awe inspired
in collective experience.
Another drive
another destination
another desert
Mojave with its legacy
of blistering heat.
Death Valley below sea level
menacingly inviting
wilderness and oases springs
exotic names

Stovepipe Wells, Furnace Creek
and Scotty's Castle - damaged
by recent floods.
Dante's view of salt flats
the Badlands - psoriatic eruptions
on desiccated plains.
Hills coiffured in corn-cobs
Zabriskie Point serene
layers of rock
on eroded mountains
telling the tales
of geological turmoil
chemicals of different
oxidation, creating
an artist's palette
nature dabbling in art.
Sand-dunes shifting hills
patterns defined by
amorous winds
hugging protrusions sandy.
Mesquite and Paramint
a trove of treasure
cradled in Neolithic land
man feeling miniscule
but spirit and imagination grand.

C 32
Hershey Falls

The charisma of camping
gear stuffed in rented van
heading north
the Grapevine
San Joaquin Valley
back roads through
citrus laden orchards
heading towards
Lake Isabella
Kern River thundering
nourishing the cornucopia
that is California.

Giant Redwoods
Sequoias of King's Canyon
laboring up,
with Mother in tow
the stone carved steps
of Moro Rock
scenic vista
the Great Western Divide
Sierra Nevada Range
peaks
with vestiges of snow
cuddling ribbons of cloud
in a sky azure.

The Yosemite Valley
elegance of
an ascending vista
painted by nature
hiding secrets
sites preserved
for posterity.

Tents pitched
sleeping bags unfurled
camp fire lit
fruit fresh from farms
left-overs warmed
shared stories over dinner.
Sleepless night
hard ground
and incessant cold -
masochistic pleasures
of the outdoor experience.
Shaver Lake
in the High Sierras
sun splashed serenity
a new dawn
refreshing walk
before packing off.

A chance stopping
water spotted
by younger sister
lunch by the riverside
spontaneous rocky slide

into a natural pool
playfully named
Hershey Falls
as we frolic
in the cooling water.

Forests left behind
dusty drive through
a comatose Bakersfield
Tejon Pass and Gorman
before descending
into the L.A. Basin
and the grind
of routine.

C 33
Father's Day

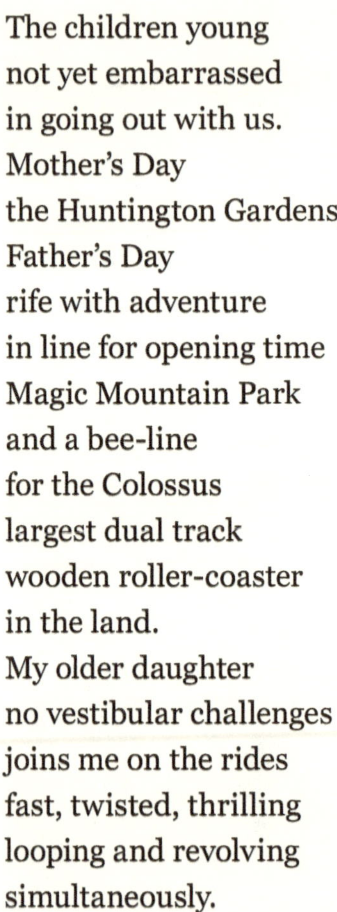

The children young
not yet embarrassed
in going out with us.
Mother's Day
the Huntington Gardens,
Father's Day
rife with adventure
in line for opening time
Magic Mountain Park
and a bee-line
for the Colossus
largest dual track
wooden roller-coaster
in the land.
My older daughter
no vestibular challenges
joins me on the rides
fast, twisted, thrilling
looping and revolving
simultaneously.

Falling freely
down a tower tall
spinning, pinned
inside the cage
of a centrifugal disc

and rising to churn
the stomach and
rattle the joints.

Walking tires
resting on low
stone walls
ears of corn
on the cob
lemonade pink.

Winning cheap
stuffed toys
to the children's
delight
pistols and rifles rigged
targets pinging
balloons filling rapidly
with jets of water
more prizes
in the offing.

The thrill
of the rides
satiated,
the desire
for stuffed toys
satisfied
no more Magic Mountain
quiet time
family time
now the forte.

C 34
Bollywood Saga

I

The stars
larger than life
on the silver screen
heroes from another era
singing ballads of love
enacting scenes
of romance
comedic interludes
pranks puerile
antics of sword and sorcery
riding and fencing
somersaulting
pole-vaulting
and beating the villains
to a pulp -
all to enthusiastic applause
and whistles wild.

K L Saigal playing emperor
singing star in drunken stupor
Motilal and Prithviraj
thunderously dramatic
Ashok Kumar at the cusp of transition
Dilip Kumar, prince of the mumble

Dev Anand, stylized star suave
Raj Kapoor the bumbling simpleton
Rajendra Kumar forever teary-eyed
and Shammi Kapoor dancing
with loose-limbed abandon.
Meena the queen of tragic roles
Madhubala of the bewitching smile
Nargis, sophistication incarnate
Asha Parekh dismissively tossing tresses
Waheeda cultured in her poise
Sadhana launching a million new coiffures
Vyjayanthimala a bundle of Tamil charm
Nimmi and Shyama
Nadira and Nighar
Nutan silently volumes expressing.

A new age, new faces
the phenomenon in Rajesh
the baritone of Amitabh
the bombastic Shatrughana
the Adonis in Dharmendra
the Jumping Jack Jitendra
the ascent of the Khans
the hidden hand of the Dons
the nibbles at stardom
of transient star scions -
of Sharmila and Saira
paving the way
for Urmila and Karisma,
Deepika and Kareena
Priyanka and Katrina

and the delicate grace
of Madhuri and Aishwarya.

The simplicity of telling tales
the landscape of common life
ceding to locales foreign
glamor replacing reality
gymnastics masquerading
as dance
and the cacophony
of clanging platters
music in the idiom modern.

The golden age of Bollywood
of dynamic stars
rendering characters stellar
fading into the sunset.

II

My parents
talked exuberantly
of the 40's Anmol Ghadi,
crooned its soulful songs
used it as a yard stick
to gauge films future.
My parents
wound up the phonograph
listening to 78 rpm discs,
Saigal or K. C. Dey
Pankaj Mullik or C.H. Atma -
orchestration minimal

for effect maximal
of soothing inflection.

My generation idolized
super-stars becoming phenomena
the airwaves replete
melody became king
the stars personified dreams
which we pursued to fulfill
in the scintillating world
of Indian cinema.

An age of remakes
piracy rediscovered
launched new starlets
defined new heroes,
pumped up
with anabolic steroids,
won new fans as
the generation millennial,
fast paced and goal oriented
relished the non-substance
of boiler plate movies
from Mumbai err Bollywood,
the misnomer
sticking in the caw,
in all plagiarized notoriety
epitomizing performances plastic
disposable easily
in an era
of attenuated attention span

and screaming fans
hugging the multiplexes.

But fading stars
left behind an aura
the tail of the comet
particles trailed
chips of the old block,
re-emergence of
talent raw, polished
as performances refined
despite contamination
from nepotism vile.
Ranveer skated
on thin ice
Ranbir consummate in method,
Akshaya mesmerized the masses
Devgan a brand created,
Hritik and Prabhu
dancers sensational
Varun and Sidharth
taming the teens,
Vicky Kaushal and
Ayushman unconventional
catapulted to stardom
in roles requiring
histrionics and athleticism.

Priyanka winning
awards at home
migrated to Hollywood

in potential eclipse
of career promising.
Aishwarya bound by scruples
missed the boat international;
Katrina charmed
her way to the top
as Parineeti, cheeky and chirpy
the girl next-door
commanded demand.

I can watch and re-watch
DVDs of Dilip and Dev and Raj;
of Amitabh and Rajesh
of Shammi with Saira,
Rajendra with Sadhana
Dharmendra and Hema -
Bollywood through its saga
catering to the taste
of the classes and
the masses eternal.

C 35
Song Of Krishna

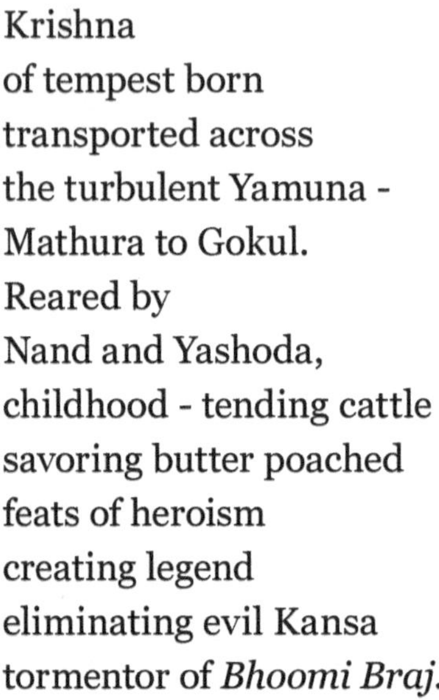

Krishna
of tempest born
transported across
the turbulent Yamuna -
Mathura to Gokul.
Reared by
Nand and Yashoda,
childhood - tending cattle
savoring butter poached
feats of heroism
creating legend
eliminating evil Kansa
tormentor of *Bhoomi Braj.*

Krishna
teaser of *Gopis*
milkmaids of the
herding tribe
granting esoteric endearment
to attendees 108
each content in
total immersion
in the Lord.
Dancing on
the moonlit meadow
banks of the River Yamuna
enchanted forest - Vrinda Van.

Krishna
of opulence mystical
enchanting with his flute
Radha a devotee
manifestation
of spirituality divine.

Krishna
human *avatar* of Vishnu
reincarnated to restore
righteousness
to a society
contaminated at its core
manipulating events
and actors
to accomplish
his agenda.

Krishna
loyal friend
guiding charioteer
spurring Arjuna
on the battlefield
at Kurukshetra.
Reciting the Gita
celestial song of Krishna
advice on the nature of life
ethics and morality
ethereal state
of body impermanent
the infinity of the soul

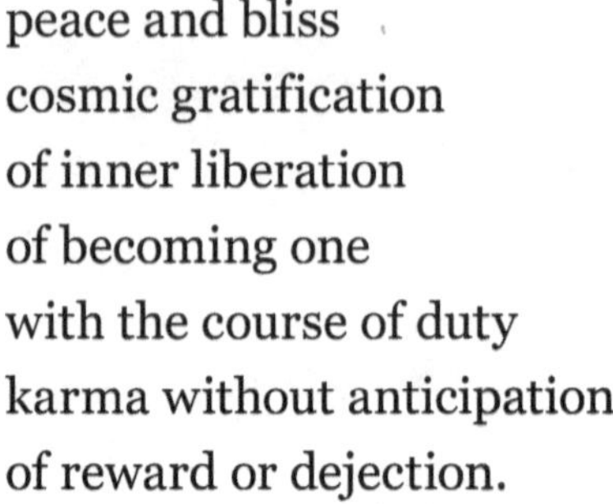

peace and bliss
cosmic gratification
of inner liberation
of becoming one
with the course of duty
karma without anticipation
of reward or dejection.

Krishna
the communicator
Krishna
the conqueror
of hearts
and minds
present as
cosmic force
the axis
of life's revolution.

C 36
Muse #12

Terraced housing
near the temple Himalayan,
your window over-looking
the square
where flower sellers
and street vendors
hawked little platters
of dried *chinar* leaves -
paraphernalia
for the rituals
of worship.

You sat there
at the window
relishing the colors
and the music
of the square below -
pretty countenance
innocent in its simplicity
mirthful eyes
a wisp of a smile
on luscious lips.
My movement was arrested
I leaned against
a *chinar* tree

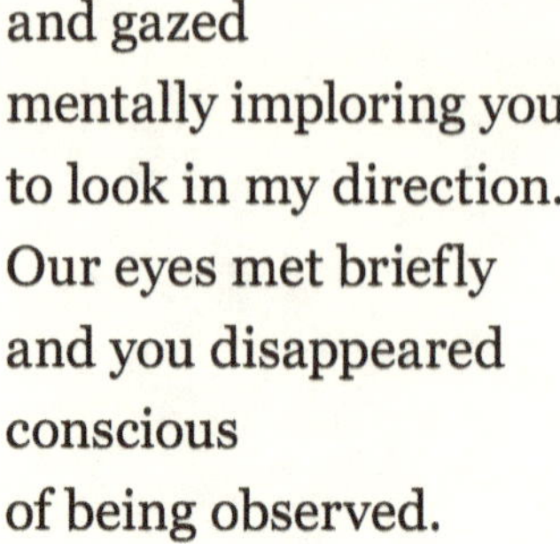

and gazed
mentally imploring you
to look in my direction.
Our eyes met briefly
and you disappeared
conscious
of being observed.

My resolve was strong
it willed you
into coming out
albeit in the company
of a younger companion.
A conversation ensued
introductions made.
It was pre-ordained
that we be together
and our grandchildren
always regaled
by the story
of how first
we met.

GLOSSARY

Achaar	pickle
Aham Brahmasmi	I am divine
Ahamkara	ego or egotism
Avatars	incarnations of a Hindu deity
Bhagwan	God; the totality of the cosmos
Bhoomi Braj	land on both sides of the Yamuna River associated with Krishna
Brahmi booti	the herb bacopa Monnieri, having medicinal properties
Bui-bui	a veiled robe worn over the clothes by Arab women
Chakras	wheels of energy through the body
Chinar	a deciduous tree found in the cold regions of the world, mainly in the Kashmir valley
Darshanas	the beholding of a deity, revered person or sacred object
Dhoti	a garment worn by male Hindus
Día de Muertos	Day of the Dead
Diyas	oil lamps usually made from clay, with cotton wicks
El Niño	a weather pattern of a warm Pacific Ocean that causes more rain than usual
Ghazals	poetic forms consisting of rhyming couplets and a refrain

Gopis	female cowherds, lovers of Krishna
Har ki Pauri	famous river landing steps on the banks of the Ganges in Haridwar
Hari-har	the supreme Absolute, after the amalgamation of Vishnu (Hari), and Shiva (Har)
Hiranya Garbha	the golden womb, source of the creation of the universe. Also, the womb of fire akin to the Big Bang
Jamuns	Indian blackberries or Java plums
Jyotirlingas	radiant signs of the Supreme God Shiva
Kabaddi	a contact team sport of Indian origin.
Kasoras	small earthenware cups
Kikapu	a handmade reed basket
Kipandes	identity documents in Kenya under British rule
Ksheer saagar	otherworldly ocean of milk
Kush grass	a grass of India used in Hindu ceremonies and for swamp coolers
Maha Mrityunjaya	a death-conquering mantra from the Rigveda
Maidan	an open square in or near a town
Malas	sets of 108 beads used while chanting mantras
Martand	literally the sun; name of an Urdu magazine
Masala	spice

Mojigangas	large puppets with the head and chest made of papier mache, supported on a wooden frame, typically farcical, exaggerated expressions, used at weddings and other major events in and around San Miguel, Mexico
Murram	a form of laterite used for road surfaces in tropical Africa and India
Nakshatras	the zodiac and heavenly asterisms
Pandit	priest
Pangas	machetes
Parathas	pan-fried Indian flatbreads
Pepeta	tamarind-plum; a fuzzy tropical fruit
Prakriti	literal - nature. The prime material energy of which all matter is composed; material nature in its germinal state; matter giving meaning to existence
Pralaya	a period of destruction of the manifested universe
Purusha	a cosmic being or self, supreme consciousness and universal principle, attributing meaning to life
Rudraksha	a seed used as a prayer bead in Hinduism
Rungus	iron-headed clubs
Sat Chita Anand	truth, consciousness, bliss; subjective experience of the ultimate, unchanging reality, called Brahman in Hindu philosophy
Shambas	small farming plots

Shesh naaga	king of all serpents; thousand-headed serpent, resting couch for Lord Vishnu, which holds the entire spherical earth on its head
Shikara	a houseboat in Kashmir
Shivalingas	representations of the male and female reproductive organs in a state of bliss; combination of the body and soul
Shivani	voice of Shiva
Sitar	a long-necked Indian stringed instrument
Tandava	divine dance of destruction performed by Hindu gods
Uhuru	freedom; liberty
Veena	an Indian stringed instrument
Vastu purusha	Lord of space
Vishwarupa	cosmic being; the supreme form of Vishnu
Yog Nidra	celestial sleep
Yug purusha	Lord of time

ACKNOWLEDGEMENTS

This anthology of poetry was made possible through the assistance and inspiration of many.

I have dedicated this collection to the legendary Indian thespian, Dev Anand who, for forty-five years, enriched my life and indeed became a member of our family. His blessings, as my mentor, my friend, my 'brother,' and a father-figure, have always sustained me through life.

I would be remiss without expressing my gratitude to my friend of almost fifty years - Parikshat Sahni – who wrote the Foreword for this volume of poetry and he deserves a poem in his own right:

PARIKSHAT

Scion of a legend
Carving
A niche
For himself,
Succeeding,
A sincere force
On the screen
And forcefully sincere
In life,

Friend and adviser
In the convoluted
Matrix of life,
Mining from experience -
Wealth garnered
Through education vast
And learning
From introspective
Scrutiny.
Grateful
That you shot
A film
In the Valley
And that
Our paths converged.

My wife Kiran and daughter Devika gave encouragement and valuable input and were an ideal sounding board for my ideas. I am grateful to my daughter Mala for designing the Chapter introduction pages and for the concept for the cover which was designed by my son-in-law, Tommy Janka, who also took my photograph for the back-cover.

Harshi Syal Gill, my sister and co-author on other ventures, polished this volume through her experience as a published writer and through her superlative editing skills, and incisive comments and suggestions. This volume would have been impossible without the countless hours she spent in all aspects of this production.

I am grateful to Daniel Garcia and Ross Butler, and their team at Goldentouch Press for their technical support and guiding hand in the publication.

There are real and imaginary characters who are the dramatis personae of the poems. My late parents, Samitra Devi and Dharam Pall Syal, have always been a fountainhead of knowledge and inspiration as has been my late brother Kailash Chander Syal, and they continue to galvanize me. My siblings - in addition to Harshi – Usha Kohli and Gaytri Saggar have always provided unconditional support and love and created precious moments to record and cherish.

My parents-in-law, the late Balwant Kaur and Kulbhushan Kochhar, are remembered fondly for their affection and encouragement through all my creative endeavors and having my back during trying times.

Shivani Jain Sharma, in India, provided pragmatic insight into the metaphysical mien of the subject, and her late father and my friend, Raj Kumar Jain, was a source of spiritual inspiration.

My family has absorbed in friendship certain people from my days in St. Helens, England. Margaret Mulcahy Crosbie is the honorary 'Gran-ma' for my daughters, and her husband Peter Crosbie is their beloved Uncle Pete. Sheila and Alan Houghton of Widnes have also become extended members of our family, and been a source of pleasant recollection. My mentors, who gave me a new professional start in L.A., the late Drs. Charles Marshall and John Gmelich, are affectionately remembered and acknowledged. My late aunt Santosh Magon, giving me my first home in England, has featured in the poetry, as have many others whom I cannot acknowledge individually, but who will know they are there when they read the poems.

However, in my childhood years, in addition to our neighborhood children, there was a core group of cousins that was an item together and I honor and respect the memories this "gang" created. This bunch included Parkash "Timmy", Naval, and Shushil "Gogo" Magon, Nilam, Deepak, and Sheetal Bedi, Parveen and Aruna Kapila, Arvind and Soneet Kapila, Lalita "Munni" and Meena "Dolly" Syal and my sister Harshi.

My childhood friend since the age of six, Ramesh Rattan, is still a part of my life and Dr. Virendra "Khoji" Talwar of Nairobi is my alter ego and will carry on inspiring all my artistic endeavors.

Finally, my cousin Manohar "Moni" Syal, in discussing my choice of ONE ZERO EIGHT as the title of this volume, suggested the addition of MANTRAS to it. However, I decided to stay with the original title, but the poems are indeed *mantras*.

A heartfelt gratitude to all these positivity-asserting forces in my life.